Spring

For Neil and Sandra
with thanks and love

Liturgical resources for February, March and April

including Lent and Holy Week

Ruth Burgess

www.ionabooks.com

First published 2019 by
Wild Goose Publications, 21 Carlton Court, Glasgow G5 9JP, UK,
the publishing division of the Iona Community.
Scottish Charity No. SC003794. Limited Company Reg. No. SC096243.

ISBN 978-1-84952-642-5

Cover photograph © Reana | Dreamstime.com

Overseas distribution
Australia: Willow Connection Pty Ltd, Unit 4A, 3–9 Kenneth Road, Manly Vale, NSW 2093
New Zealand: Pleroma, Higginson Street, Otane 4170, Central Hawkes Bay
Canada: Bayard Distribution, 10 Lower Spadina Ave., Suite 400, Toronto, Ontario M5V 2Z

Printed by Bell & Bain, Thornliebank, Glasgow

Contents

Introduction 15

Spring in February 17

Candlemas 23

Fair Trade Fortnight 35

Ash Wednesday 41

Resources for Lent: Common Lectionary Year A 63

Resources for Lent: Common Lectionary Year B 77

Resources for Lent: Common Lectionary Year C 99

General resources for Lent 127

Annunciation 139

Mothering Sunday 145

Spring in March 155

Palm Sunday 165

Palm Sunday Evening 183

Monday, Tuesday and Wednesday of Holy Week 191

Maundy Thursday 209

Gethsemane 235

Good Friday 247

Holy Saturday 273

Easter Vigil 281

Easter Morning 287

Earth Day 313

Spring in April 317

The earth awakens 327

About the authors 335

Index of authors 341

Contents in detail

Introduction 15

Spring in February 17

- The coming of spring 18
- St Bridget 18
- As the days lengthen 19
- Through frozen ground 20
- February is blessed 21

Candlemas 23

- Old folk 24
- A couple came in with their baby 25
- My name is Anna 28
- Joseph (Luke 2:22–38) 29
- God's blessing (Luke 2:39–40) 30
- God of light and love 31
- Nunc Dimittis 1 32
- Nunc Dimittis 2 33

Fair Trade Fortnight 35

- To love God is to love each other (A song for Sally) 36
- Ordinary tea 38

Ash Wednesday 41

- Ash Wednesday Eve (Shrove Tuesday) 42
- Collect for Ash Wednesday (Isaiah 58:1–12) 43
- Remember that you are dust 43
- The time for ashing 44
- An Ash Wednesday service 45
- Have compassion on us: An Ash Wednesday liturgy 52
- We don't like Ash Wednesday 56
- Help us turn 57

Key to symbols

- Prayer
- Biblical reflection
- Liturgy
- Song
- Story
- Script
- Meditation
- Reflection
- Poem
- Responsive prayer
- Monologue
- U Child-friendly

Your mercy is so huge (Psalm 51) 58
Companions 60

Resources for Lent: Common Lectionary Year A 63

Collects for Lent 64
U I am long and very slithery (Genesis 2 and 3) 66
The unexpected move (Genesis 12:1–9) 69
U Abram and Sarai (Genesis 12) 70
Nicodemus' song (John 3) 71
U Whoosh! Gurgle! Splossshhh! (Exodus 17) 72
I do not judge as you judge (1 Samuel 16) 73
Dem bones, dem bones (Ezekiel 37) 74

Resources for Lent: Common Lectionary Year B 77

U I saw a dove (Mark 1:9–15) 78
Baptism 79
U I wonder (Mark 1:9–15) 80
I put my trust (Psalm 25) 81
We bring to God 83
We come to you with wonder and awe (Psalm 22:23–31) 84
For generations (John 2:13–22) 86
U Mr Nice Guy (John 2:13–17) 87
What kind of Saviour? 88
God of passion 88
U Your glory fills the heavens (Psalm 19) 89
Lifted up (John 3:14–21) 91
We come to you (Psalm 107:1–3,17–22) 92
This is the truth (John 12:20–33) 94
You show us how to let go (John 12:20–33) 95
We who gather (Psalm 119:9–16) 96

Resources for Lent: Common Lectionary Year C 99

U In the desert (Luke 4:1–13) 100
U Forty days 101

(Responsive prayer) You're my refuge (Psalm 91) 102
(Story) U Foxes and hens (Luke 13:31–35) 105
(Song) Lament for Jerusalem (and other cities) 107
(Responsive prayer) Light and deliverance (Psalm 27) 108
(Story) Second chance (Luke 13:1–9) 110
(Script) U The master is coming tomorrow (Luke 13:1–9) 111
(Responsive prayer) I search for you (Psalm 63) 113
(Script) Lost and found (Luke 15:11–32) 115
(Reflection) Who would have thought? 118
(Responsive prayer) Telling you everything (Psalm 32) 119
(Script) Lazarus and Martha reflect (John 12:1–8) 121
(Prayer) Around a table 123
(Responsive prayer) Filled with laughter (Psalm 126) 124

General resources for Lent 127

(Reflection) Rethinking Lent 128
(Story) U Clare's grandad (A children's story about death) 131
(Reflection) A season for more 133
(Reflection) A long forty days of silence 134
(Prayer) It's easy to say sorry 134
(Prayer) Dear God 136
(Reflection) This is the season 137

Annunciation 139

(Story) U Mary 140
(Reflection) I wanted to say no 140
(Poem) The morning began quietly 142
(Reflection) Waiting 142

Mothering Sunday 145

(Prayer) Christ who loves us 146
(Song) Mothering God 146
(Prayer) We lift our prayers to you 147
(Prayer) Sticky fingers, sloppy kisses 148

Key to symbols

(cross)	Prayer
(cross-flower)	Biblical reflection
(liturgy)	Liturgy
♫	Song
(story)	Story
(mask)	Script
♥	Meditation
(window)	Reflection
(poem)	Poem
((O))	Responsive prayer
●	Monologue
U	Child-friendly

((◎)) We pray for God's family 149
✝ Sometimes it's tough being a parent 150
✗ Unsung 151
✝ In my beginning 151
((◎)) Mothering Sunday prayers 152
✝ We pray also 154

Spring in March 155

✗ Primroses on the Uisken road 156
♥ One more spring 156
✝ Creator God 157
♫ I wake and know (St Patrick) 158
● Joseph 160
♫ A song for St Cuthbert's Holy Island 160
✗ Wake 161
⊞ The new growth of spring 162
⊞ A second chance 163

Palm Sunday 165

● An arrangement 166
♫ U Children's song 167
✝ Palm Sunday collect 168
● So many journeys 168
☺ Here we go 169
☺ U Script for eleven voices (Luke 19:28–40) 171
☺ U Mum, I'm hungry (a script for two voices) 176
☺ U Are you coming? 178
⊞ If our Queen rode a donkey 180
✝ Let us journey with you 181
✝ A blessing of palm crosses 182

Palm Sunday Evening 183

♫ We see the crowds 184
((◎)) After the palms and the parade 185

U A child's-eye view 187
Let's stay with the Hosannas 189
Jesus needs his friends (a sending) 190

Monday, Tuesday and Wednesday of Holy Week 191

Three liturgies 192
Remember her, remember me 198
Extravagant love (John 12:1–8) 200
What a waste 201
Come Monday, Tuesday, Wednesday 202
Well done, Judas 205

Maundy Thursday 209

All is set 210
Come Thursday 211
Here we are 212
Feet 213
Foot washing – three takes 214
A night of wonder (John 13:1–17) 216
Let you wash my feet! (John 13:1–15) 218
Here is a table 218
Peter's story 226
Radical 232
Judas reflects 233

Gethsemane 235

We should have been there for him 236
Watch with me 237
At midnight in a garden 238
In Gethsemane 240
Take this cup away from me (Luke 22:42) 240
In the courtyard (John 18:12–27) 244
Wine is poured and bread is broken
(A hymn for Maundy Thursday) 246

Good Friday 247

Reflection — Come Friday 248
Liturgy, Child-friendly — Good Friday (an all-age service) 249
Prayer — This is the day we dread 254
Reflection — Hands of Jesus 255
Meditation — If God does not weep 256
Script — Who gets into paradise? (Luke 23:32–43) 257
Story — The Red Road 258
Monologue — The sister of Mary 263
Monologue — The worst of it 264
Poem — Blood and bone 266
Reflection — How dare the cross? 266
Poem — Good Friday in any town 267
Prayer — Postmodern 268
Reflection, Child-friendly — The good guy 269
Reflection — Judas 270
Poem — Pietà 271
Monologue — Nicodemus 272

Holy Saturday 273

Reflection — Come Saturday 274
Liturgy, Child-friendly — A service in a graveyard 275
Reflection — Why is it holy? 277
Reflection — An aching place 278
Poem — Piercings 278
Reflection — Holy Saturday is longer than a day 280

Easter Vigil 281

Reflection — Get ready 282
Reflection — Dying to life 282
Responsive prayer — You have brought us from darkness into light (an Easter Vigil prayer of thanksgiving) 283
Responsive prayer — The light keeps getting brighter now 285

Key to symbols

- Prayer
- Biblical reflection
- Liturgy
- Song
- Story
- Script
- Meditation
- Reflection
- Poem
- Responsive prayer
- Monologue
- U — Child-friendly

Easter Morning 287

Darkness before dawn 288
Birds still sing 288
A gathering prayer 289
The angel 290
Spinning the story 291
Easter according to John's Gospel 293
Mad Mary 299
Conversation with a gardener 304
Resurrection 305
An Easter prayer of confession 305
An Easter morning communion 306
Responses before the Gospel reading 309
We do not claim to understand 309
U He is with us forever 310
Thank you 311

Earth Day 313

God of new life 314
A climate of change 314
The silent witness of the heavens 315
Each day another species lost forever 316

Spring in April 317

The light of day 318
I look with compassion 318
Upside-down God 319
Yangtze Easter 320
This year's diary 321
U Thank you, God, for spring 322
If we wait 322
Resurrection and love 324
Spring swings 324

Burgeoning 325
Sacrament 326
Help us to know ourselves 326

The earth awakens 327

A liturgy for spring 328
An elemental blessing 332

About the authors 335
Index of authors 341

Key to symbols

Prayer
Biblical reflection
Liturgy
Song
Story
Script
Meditation
Reflection
Poem
Responsive prayer
Monologue
U Child-friendly

Introduction

Spring follows *Winter.*

Spring is a liturgical resource book that covers the months of February, March and April. It includes prayers, responses, stories, songs, poems, liturgies, reflections, scripts and monologues for the major Christian festivals and fast days of Lent and Holy Week, as well as for Candlemas, Fair Trade Fortnight and Earth Day. The material is written by Iona Community members, associates, friends and others.

I've defined each season by the month that contains the solstice or equinox and the month either side of it.

As the date of Easter changes each year I have chosen to include material for Easter and Eastertide in the next volume of this series, *Summer.*

Thank you to all the contributors for their rich and imaginative material that I have been privileged to edit.

Given the quality and amount of material that was contributed to this book and its predecessor *Winter*, completing the series in due course, with *Summer* and *Autumn*, should be a pleasure and a delight.

Thank you, too, to the Wild Goose Publications team: Maria O'Neill, Jane Darroch Riley for their professionalism and support – and particularly thank you to Sandra Kramer and Neil Paynter.

Bless to us, O God,
the fragility of snowdrops,
the blossoming of orchards,
the dancing of bees.

Bless to us, O God,
the wriggling of tadpoles,
the shedding of Damart,*
the lengthening of days.

Bless to us, O God,
the smudge of ashes,
the Lenten journey,
the blazing Easter fire.

Bless and silence us with wonder,
O God of hope and justice.
Gift us with courage.
Warm and quicken us with love.

Ruth Burgess

*winter underwear

Spring in February

The coming of spring

Beneath frost-hardened ground
myriad bulbs start to swell,
developing root systems
unseen.

Through a covering of snow,
shoots slowly push their way
foretelling the sure approach
of spring.

Soon the sun's tentative rays
filter through wintry skies,
and growing buds respond to
their warmth.

Then we glimpse snowdrops
and swathes of crocuses,
sense winter is almost past …
and smile.

Kathy Crawford

St Bridget

She wove with reeds,
plaiting the green fronds.
Warp and weft dovetailed,
blended, welded,
knotted and twined,
till a cross was made;

four green arms
to touch the world.
She tied ribbons there,
blue or green maybe;

small bows that
curtseyed to the world.

She walked around
and gave a cross here,
a cross there, blessed
with love, the love
of God for the world.

They hang now by hearth
and range, in kitchen,
stall and hallway,
to move the hearts of
traveller and tramp,
of granny and gramps;

to stir with love,
to speak of welcome,
to embrace the poor,
to invite angels to the dance.

Judy Dinnen

As the days lengthen

Alpha and Omega, you were there at our beginning
and you will be there at our end.
Coasts and islands wait for the dawn,
the dark sea surrounds us like waters in the womb,
like the last river we have to cross.
We wait, trusting, seeing the sky lightening, horizons opening up,
colours of dawn dancing across restless waves.

Spirit of God, in Jesus, you shared our birth and our mortality,
and you are present with us now. We wait.
The clouds become bright, the rocks glow,
our hearts catch fire with sudden joy – the sun rises.
Rise in our hearts, we pray, today and every day.

God of creation, you greet us every new day,
and, as the days lengthen, we see green shoots of spring;
snowdrops, faithful in their presence year by year;
lengthening days and sunlit moments,
all these speak to us of your love.
We praise you for these signs of your life-giving Spirit
and for Jesus, who embodied that love,
who came to share our human lives,
calling men and women to follow him,
and to be salt and light in their communities;
Jesus who listened and shared meals, taught and healed,
walked country tracks and city streets in the land that we call Holy;
who kept the faith and challenged apathy and abuse of power;
who was rejected and reviled, tortured and nailed to a cross.
Who died.
And who rose again, like the sun in the morning,
so all the world can see that your love is stronger than death.
We praise you now in the power of the Spirit,
enlivening, encouraging – and present with us now. Amen

Jan Sutch Pickard

Through frozen ground

The seed lies dormant
in frozen ground,
waiting for spring rains
to filter through with hope,
waiting for the light,
waiting for warm winds and summer sun
to thaw the frigid earth.

Waiting,
lying dormant while other seeds begin to grow
and other soil is turned.
Still sleeping it waits
as new seeds are scattered.

Waiting always waiting,
as the rising sun and falling moon make their rounds.

Waiting,
the seed does not beg for growth
only waits for new life to awaken.
Rains come and winds blow,
sun shines,
and the seed senses something stirring.

Filled with desire for what lies ahead,
waiting gives way to a new day;
touched by light,
growing among other seeds,
dormant no longer,
new life comes
through frozen ground.

Rebeka Maples

February is blessed

Still bleak and wintery
February is blessed
with winter-white snowdrops
and carpets of colourful crocuses.

Under the earth creatures stir
as more light brightens
the still short days.

Trees are bare
but new life is within them
waiting
silently waiting.
Lent will come soon,
a spring-cleaning for our souls.

In our times of terror,
towering infernos
and glaring inequalities,
we long for better to come.

May God bless us with
February rainbows,
a St David's Day of yellow daffodils,
a promise of love,
a revival of life.

Sarah Pascoe

Candlemas

Old folk

Have you heard the latest about that batty old Anna?

You know – that old woman who thinks she's a prophetess. Wanders round the Temple all day, praying all over the place. Eighty-four if she's a day! Don't know how she's managed to live to that age – not with all her problems.

Did you realise that she's been a widow for years and years?

It's true. She married this man who only managed to survive for seven years, and then he died and left her on her own. Mind you, if she's always been as strange as she is now, maybe that had something to do with it.

Anyway, I was telling you the latest.

Apparently this nice young couple had brought their baby to the Temple to be dedicated. Firstborn boy, you see. Everybody has to do it. And they'd already had an encounter with that other strange character – Simeon, they call him. He's one of those weird people who still believe the Messiah will come. Only he's a bit more peculiar than the others because he believes it will happen before he dies. And it appears that he thinks that day has finally arrived. I ask you!

Well, anyway, this young couple had just recovered from him praying and praising God all over their baby, when they turned round, and there was Anna lying in wait for them. They certainly had their fill of odd experiences that morning.

She didn't exactly leap out at them. Well, you wouldn't at her age, would you? But she certainly made sure they couldn't get past her until she'd said her piece. At first I think they just thought she was one of those old dears who drool all over babies and say stupid things about how much they look like their fathers or mothers. But she took one look and then started off on one of her praising God sessions and telling anybody who would listen that this child was a special one promised by God.

I ask you, those poor parents must have been lost for words. One old man tells them they've given birth to the Messiah, so he can now die happy, and an even older woman starts telling the same story to anyone who couldn't avoid her fast enough.

What a day they must have had. I'll bet they'll never forget it. It must be the strangest experience they'll ever have in their lives.

But what do old people know about anything? They're just out of date and past it. They live in a world of their own, while the rest of us get on with our business.

It's such a stupid idea.

Fancy thinking that a child can make any difference! Whoever heard of such a thing?

Marjorie Dobson

A couple came in with their baby

I stood in the Temple courtyard,
waiting.
I was not really sure why, or for what.
I just knew I needed to be there
in that particular place,
at that particular time.

A couple came in with their baby.
They said they had come for a Presentation ritual,
so he was obviously their first son.
I greeted them.
The man told me they wanted to sacrifice two doves or pigeons.
I nodded, understandingly.
The family must be quite poor, I thought.
That was the cheaper option for those who could not afford
a lamb or goat.

I asked their names.
'Joseph and Mary,' the man answered.

'And the baby's name?'
'Jesus,' said his mother proudly.
Quite an unusual name that. I wondered why they chose it.
It means Saviour.

'Where do you come from?' I asked.
'Nazareth originally, but Jesus was born in Bethlehem,' said Joseph.
'Why Bethlehem?' I enquired.

Voice: someone out of sight reads Micah 5:2:

God said, Bethlehem, you are one of the smallest towns in Judah,
but out of you I will bring a ruler for Israel …

'Because Joseph is descended from King David,' Mary answered.
'We had to go there for the recent census.'

I carefully held the sleeping baby in my arms and gazed at his face.

Voice: Isaiah 9:6–7:

A child is born to us, a son is given to us and he will be our ruler …
He will rule with right and justice from now until the end of time.

Was it possible that the ancient prophecies were being fulfilled at last?
Had the event I had prayed about so often taken place during my lifetime?
The clues were all there. Surely this baby was the Messiah!
With joy in my heart – and a big smile on my face – I blessed him.
Then I handed Jesus back to his parents.

Other prophecies soon came into my mind.
The ones from Isaiah about how the Messiah would suffer.

Voice: Isaiah 53:6:

Like lost sheep, we went astray. He suffered for us. He was in pain.
And we thought his suffering was a punishment from God.

I told Mary about them as gently as I could.
She nodded and seemed to understand.
Mary looked so young,

but there was a maturity about her which was way beyond her years;
I detected strength of character too.
I think my words confirmed what others had already told her.
Mary began to tell me about the visit from the Angel Gabriel
when she was told that she would be the mother of God's son,
and then about all the unusual events surrounding Jesus' birth.
Anna, the prophetess, must have realised what was happening.
She came across to join us.
I'd not seen her move that quickly in years!

Sometime later, the family went home
and I was left to reflect on the amazing privilege I'd been given
to welcome God's Messiah.
Anna's joy was obvious too –
she couldn't stop talking about the baby!

It was a day I'll never forget.

Voice: Luke 2:29:

Lord, now let your servant depart in peace …
with my own eyes I have seen what you promised …

Kathy Crawford

My name is Anna

My name is Anna.
Not Sarah.
She was too old too.
She was sad.
It seemed too late
to have that long-awaited heir with her loving husband, Abraham.
Then she laughed.
Then she lied.
Then she laughed again.
The son she bore was important.
He heard God's voice telling him not to be afraid,
that He would always be with him
as he took on the legacy of goods, land
and the growth of a mighty nation.
His name was Isaac.

My name is Anna.
Not Hannah.
She was barren.
She was sad.
She prayed. She pleaded.
It wasn't too late.
She had a son with her loving husband, Elkanah.
She handed her son over to the Temple
whilst singing a song of rejoicing to God.
The son she bore was important.
He heard God's voice
and spoke God's words to the nation with authority and power.
His name was Samuel.

My name is Anna.
Not Sarah.
Not Hannah.
I am old.
I am barren.
I live in a place where the God of Isaac and Samuel dwells.

I have seen the nation. I have heard the prophecies.
Now, towards the end of my life, I sing.
I sing a song of rejoicing.
I see this young woman.
The son she bore is important.
He will hear God's voice
and bring about the redemption
not only of one nation,
but of all who believe.
His name is Jesus.

Pam Hathorn

Joseph (Luke 2:22–38)

Well, the time had come to go to Jerusalem for the purification, and to present Jesus at the Temple and offer sacrifices. He's our firstborn. I wish we'd had more to offer than a pair of birds. He deserves so much more. But I'm too young to have much by way of reputation and don't have many customers, so it's all we could afford. I'm grateful that giving what we could is enough for God, even if it doesn't feel like enough to me. But then, could I ever feel like I was giving enough?

Strange, those days around his birth: that rather bizarre visit from the shepherds, and the things they said. It's still not clear to me, actually. Is he mine, or not? When I look at him I see my mother's eyes, but …

I want to do the best I can by him, for all our sakes. Mary's story … I love her, I trust her, and yet … Where do I take these questions that haunt me?

I shall make him mine. He will get as much as I can give him in love and protection. I shall train him to be a carpenter; and he will care for us in our old age. Can I put my stamp on Jesus, make him mine? …

Whilst we were offering our sacrifices a man came up to us. He said his name was Simeon and that he had waited for this moment. He took Jesus in his arms, praised God and said all sorts of astonishing things. 'A light for revelation to the Gentiles, and for glory to your people Israel.'

Oh my! On the one hand that's amazing. Apparently our little boy *really* is special. With guilt, I recognise that I enjoy the reflected glory. A nobody like me, somehow associated with *this*. Underneath that I feel disquiet: what will this mean for him? For us? What is the cost of glory?

Doubt returns. Was he ever, can he ever, truly be my son? How can a carpenter be a revelation to the Gentiles? How do I relate to this child, who is so normal, mewling and puking, yet apparently utterly other?

If I'm honest, I feel sidelined. Simeon spoke to Mary, not to me. I seem to be surplus to requirements. Will my heart not be hurt when he is hurt?

Nevertheless, I shall do my best by the lad. Can I bury my pride, my hurt, my desires, my very self, and be content with this hidden work?

Evelyn Sweerts

God's blessing (Luke 2:39-40)

O Jesus,
child,
I don't know whether to be sad or happy.

Before you were conceived
Gabriel told me that
God had blessed me.

Before you were born,
Elizabeth blessed us both.

Just now in the Temple
Simeon blessed us,
both me and Joseph.

But then he also told me
that one day something bad
would happen to you.
Something that would break
my heart.

O Jesus,
child,
what is going to happen to you
and to me
and to Joseph?

I am so scared.
I want to go home.

And when Joseph and Mary had finished doing all that the law required of them, they returned to their hometown of Nazareth, in Galilee. And Jesus grew, and became strong; he was full of wisdom, and God's blessing was upon him. (Lk 2:39–40)

Ruth Burgess

God of light and love

God of light and love,
warming February's chill,
tempering the winds,
peppering hard ground
with early shoots of green
and hints of blossom,
we lift to you
the cold bones of winter
and hearts aflame with hope.

We praise you
for the Light
that has arrived with Jesus,
shining in the darkness,
unquenchable and true.

We praise you
for the hope of his presence,
guiding our feet,

lighting our pathway,
casting warming rays
and the glow of fulfilment.

We praise you
for the discomfort
of his searchlight beams,
concealing nothing,
truth-telling,
life-changing.

Examine us and know us, O God.
Drive out the darkness,
turn our hearts to you
and fill our souls
with the song of salvation,
with the message of your love.

Holy God, we worship you!
We sing your praise
now and forever.
Amen

Louise Gough

Nunc Dimittis 1

Tune: 'Matt Hyland' (Irish traditional)

O Lord, now let your servant go
to find the peace that you have promised.
My eyes have seen your living gift:
and all the waiting years are finished.

He stands revealed for all to see,
to bring the nations peace and safety;
a light to shine for all the world
and Israel's unending glory.

Sing praise to God, who made the worlds,
and sing the Son through whom he made them,
and sing the Spirit, Lord of life,
unbounded love in light unfading.

Roddy Cowie

See: https://audioboom.com/posts/6067114-nunc-dimittis-to-matt-hyland

Nunc Dimittis 2

Tune: 'Bogie's bonnie belle' (Scottish traditional)

O Lord, now let your servant go
in confidence and peace:
your ancient promise is fulfilled,
now grant me your release.

My eyes have seen the one you raised
where all the world can see –
to lead the lost to safety
and to set the captives free.

A light to shine in distant lands
where age-long darkness fell;
the bright and promised glory
of your people Israel.

Let every voice give praise to God
and glorify his Son,
and bless the holy breath of life
till worlds and time are done.
Amen

Roddy Cowie

See: https://audioboom.com/posts/6067086-nunc-dimittis-to-bogie-s-bonnie-belle

Fair Trade Fortnight

To love God is to love each other

A song for Sally

Words and music by Ruth Bamforth

To love God is to love each other;
there are many ways to show we care,
in our homes, in our lives together,
our acts of kindness, thoughts we share.

So I wonder: who is my neighbour
in the town, the street, the house next door?
Reaching out, welcome in the stranger,
the refugee, the scared, the poor.

When the call comes, stand up for justice,
for speech that's free, for life that's fair,
for the homeless, for the migrant, shelter,
for help, for hope to lift despair.

In one world we must work together,
sharing gifts and talents, ours to give.
Celebrate all that makes us different,
yet as one people learn to live.

To love God is to love each other;
be kind, be true, keep righting wrong.
There'll be darkness, but remember laughter;
keep hope in your heart, in your voice a song.

Ruth Bamforth

Ordinary tea

We talk of an English tea party,
with tea in china cups, scones
and jam or cucumber sandwiches.

We've borrowed this infusion, called it ours.
We've domesticated it, called it 'ordinary'
or labelled it as workmen's tea,
the strong stuff that the spoon stands up in.

But look at the box it came in.
Look at the amber sky,
the russet soil,
the dark acacia trees
spreading their arms across the plain.
Look at the burnished bronze panel
with the words African Gold,
reminding us of minerals deep
below the burning earth.

Look at the pictures of pickers.
They glide through tea bushes,
expertly plucking the best leaves,
tossing them over their shoulders
into large, deep baskets.

We follow them to the factory,
see moving belts with chopped, dried leaves
travel from field to the china cup.

No it's not ours; it's not ordinary,
but a gift from hot countries,
a reminder of wide-open spaces,
mountaintops covered with bushes,
dedicated workers picking and packing,
so we can sit at the table,
or sit in the canteen,
or sit on a picnic rug in the shade
and sip our favourite brew.

Judy Dinnen

Ash Wednesday

Ash Wednesday Eve (Shrove Tuesday)

It seems like only
yesterday
they fit so
comfortably
in our palms, as
we paraded around the
sanctuary
singing our glad songs (the
teachers whispering,
'they're not *those* kind
of cymbals' when we tried
to bang them together),
and brought them up to the
front to place
on the table;

now, hushed and still,
we watch
as a flame curls around the
crunchy, dusty, dry
leaves crumbled up in
an old pot,
slowly reduced to ashes
we will put on (not
understanding why,
perhaps)
tomorrow
and wear until the day
our smudged lives
are cleansed
by the holy oil
of your
tears.

Thom M Shuman

Collect for Ash Wednesday (Isaiah 58:1–12)

O God, advocate of all who are oppressed,
you shatter our illusions of righteousness
and unmask our divided hearts,
in order that we might be filled with longing for justice and generosity
and so be made whole.
As justice for those who work,
and generosity for those who cannot,
are true marks of a heart turning towards you,
let our actions as well as our intentions
bear witness for the longing of our hearts.

Kathy Galloway

Remember that you are dust

Palm fronds,
products of so much growth and sun,
symbols of rejoicing and welcome,
burnt to ash and mixed with oil.
Such greenness reduced to a bland, pessimistic grey.

'Remember that you are dust,
and unto dust you shall return.'

It is with this we are blessed, anointed,
our weakness and mortality.

Mary Hanrahan

The time for ashing

The time for ashing has come.

The time to remember that we are dust
and to dust we shall return, dust made by God.
The time to sit with the truth
that we are created by God, in love, from the dust.

The time for ashing has come.

The time to make our fast and give our alms,
the time for stillness and quiet thought.
The time for repentance,
the time for gratitude.

The time for ashing has come.

Jenny Wilson

An Ash Wednesday service

Suggested readings:

Psalm 139:7–12; Amos 5:8–15; Luke 18:9–14; Romans 8:31–35

Call to worship:

We gather in the dimness of evening,
To be with the God who brightens
the shadows of our lives.

We gather in the quiet of this place,
To be with Jesus, knowing that nothing
past, present or future separates us.

We gather to be marked as disciples,
To be fed for the journey through Lent,
to be sealed by the Spirit as God's own.

Evening prayer:

You wait this evening,
Patient God, for us to come back:
to stop going away from you
on our self-focused travels;
to set aside our empty fears;
to cease shaping you in our image,
so we can discover you closer
than we ever dared imagine.

You wait for us this night,
Companion of our hearts,
for us to follow once more:
leaving the shuttered corners
of our lives;
refusing to go from one failed
promise to another;
coming out of the panic rooms

we have built in our souls,
so you can take us by the hand
to lead us to resurrection life.

You wait in the scattered ashes of our lives,
Spirit of silence, for us to find you:
in the broken bread
which strengthens us to serve;
in the cup of grace
which fills our emptiness;
in our sisters and brothers
who are willing to hold us up
when we falter,
so you can embrace us
with joy and hope in every moment.

As you wait, and as we seek
to return to you in these moments,
we pray as we are taught …

The Lord's Prayer

Invitation to the Lenten life:

Not for the first time, yet fresh once more,
we accompany Jesus to Jerusalem.
Because of his experience in the wilderness,
we discover how we might have the strength
to turn our back on evil, so we can choose good.

By his example of fasting and prayer
in the midst of serving and caring for others,
we can learn that rhythm of faithful living
which allows us to work for justice and hope,
as we draw strength from the timeless acts
of silence, feasting on the word and prayer.

As we remember our baptism into faith,
as we gather at the feast of grace,

as we are marked as Christ's own,
we prepare ourselves to come to God,
on this holy night.

Call to reconciliation:

On this night,
we begin our journey to Easter.
Before we can take the first step,
we must admit how we have not been faithful to our God.
Let us pray together, saying:

Unison prayer for forgiveness:

We have trouble telling the truth, God of broken hearts,
yet we must admit
on this night how we have trouble being your people.
We may not trample the poor,
but we sometimes walk right past them.
We don't receive bribes,
but we are more privileged than many around us.
We trust more in ourselves than in you,
and spend far too much time patting ourselves on the back,
rather than holding out a hand to others.

Where can we go for forgiveness but to you, God of the ashes?
When we are greedy,
you promise to be gracious.
When we have trouble confronting injustice,
you stand at our side.
When we struggle to seek good,
you point us to Jesus,
our brother, our Saviour,
who shows us how to turn our back on evil
to follow him.
Amen

Silence

Assurance of pardon:

God refuses to stand far off,
but comes close to us –
to hear our prayers,
to touch our hearts with forgiveness,
and to walk with us during this holy season and beyond.

We have no need to go anyplace else
but into the comforting and restoring heart
of the One who loves us.
Thanks be to God.
We are forgiven.
Amen

Imposition of the ashes:

Just yesterday, it seems, the palms were
fresh and green, held tight in hands
as we re-enacted Jesus' entry into Jerusalem.
But then they dried, shrivelled, became
almost too fragile to touch, until
we burned them into the ashes for tonight.
Yet, by the grace of our God,
with the Spirit resting upon them,
they are mixed with oil and placed
on our forehead or the palm of our hand,
the dust of life resting upon us
as a sign that by sharing the gifts of peace, reconciliation,
justice and generosity,
we will live into the people we long to become.

God of all moments,
touch us with the ashes of repentance.
Mark us with your forgiveness and grace.

Folk may come to have the sign of the cross placed on their forehead or palm.

Invitation to the Table

The Great Prayer of thanksgiving:

May the God of the ashes be with you.
And also with you.

On this night, let us offer our hearts to God.
We open them so we may be filled with the gifts of Lenten discipleship.

Let us lift glad thanksgiving to our God.
We offer praise to the One who gives us the strength for this journey.

There at the edge of the emptiness of chaos
you spoke, God of all graciousness,
brightening the shadows with lights in the sky,
pouring the waters into rivers and seas,
planting seeds to feed all creatures.

From the dust of creation, you shaped your children,
offering us all the goodness and beauty
which overflowed from your heart,
but we trampled through your hopes,
as we turned from your heart
to chase after evil's false promises.

But no matter where we went,
or how far we sought to flee from you,
you continued to meet us in all those places,
constantly inviting us to return to you
and be filled with your steadfast love.

Therefore, in the silence and shadows of this evening,
we join with our sisters and brothers
to offer you songs of thanksgiving:

Holy, holy, holy are you, God who is at our side.
We join all creation in singing your praises.
Hosanna in the highest!

Blessed is the One who makes us right.
Hosanna in the highest!

Your constant love is the seal of your holiness,
and Jesus is the One who comes
so we will never be separated from you.
He endured every hardship we experience,
so we receive the hope you offer to us;
he experienced the hunger of loneliness,
so we might become members of your family;
he was willing to set aside his life,
so death would have no power
to keep us apart from you, but
your resurrection power would give us
the same life he received from you.

As we take our tentative first steps towards Jerusalem,
as we are marked as his companions,
we remember that mystery known as faith:

Christ died, not withholding his heart.
Christ was raised, so that he might become our advocate.
Christ will come, to draw us to your side.

Here at this Table of life and longing,
pour out your Spirit on us,
and on the gifts offered to us.
May the bread which is broken
strengthen us so nothing can separate us
from those who struggle with life,
from those who mourn a death,
from those who have no power or voice.

May the cup which overflows with grace
nourish us so we pick up
those who have been trampled by misery,
those who are trapped by injustice,
those who are pushed aside by the privileged.

And when neither death nor life
can keep us apart from you,
as you gather us around your Table
with our sisters and brothers,
we will sing your glory and praise forever and ever,
God in Community, Holy and One.
Amen

Sending:

Smudged this night with the ashes of penitence,
We will go out to share God's forgiveness
with those we have hurt, with those who are forgotten.

Fed this night by the Host of the Feast of grace,
We will go out to bring healing to the broken,
to offer grace to those trampled by the powerful.

Called this night to journey through suffering to new life,
We will go out to stand with those experiencing injustice,
to share the Spirit's peace and reconciliation with the world.

Thom M Shuman

Have compassion on us: An Ash Wednesday liturgy

Notes:

Have three stations set up around the building. At station one you will need a person to hold the ashes and a person to distribute them. At station two, a person to smooth the sand and say the words of Jesus. At station three, a person to sprinkle the water and to say the words (see An invitation to act).

Opening responses:

In your loving kindness,
Have compassion on us, God.

You want us to be honest.
Have compassion on us, God.

You invite us to tell the truth.
Have compassion on us, God.

You want to wash us clean.
Have compassion on us, God.

Have compassion on us, O God,
As we return to you.

Song

Prayer of approach:

God of love and hope and life,
at the beginning of Lent
we come to you.

You know who we are.
You know what we are like.
You know what is important to us.
You know where we hurt.

We come to you seeking forgiveness.
We come to you seeking strength for our journey.
We come to you seeking love.

God of love and hope and life,
meet us here.
Amen

Reading: **Psalm 51:1–13 (a modern version)**

A short silence

Reading: **Matthew 18:1–9**

Reflection:

A child.
Jesus put a child in the middle of them:
a little child.
A child with sticky fingers.
A child with grubby knees.
A child with her hair all over the place.
A laughing child.
A child in tears.

You need to change, said Jesus to the adults.
Become like a little child.
Not childish
but childlike.
Enjoy life.
Take risks.
Make mistakes.
Laugh and cry.
Say you're sorry and start again.

And look after the children, said Jesus.
All the little ones
and the vulnerable ones.

Don't let them be bullied.
Don't let them get hurt.
Don't hurt them yourself.
The worst thing you can do is
to hurt those who are vulnerable.
The worst thing you can do is
let those who are vulnerable believe that they are not loved.

In this world,
on this earth,
today and tomorrow,
if you are tempted to turn away from the love of Jesus
you need to turn around.

A short period of music for reflection

Song

An invitation to act:

Music will play for 15 minutes. You are invited to visit the three stations around the building:

Station 1

The imposition of ashes: an ancient Christian symbol of repentance and a reminder of our human condition. You are invited to come forward and ashes will be placed on your hand or forehead in the sign of the cross, accompanied with these words:

'Remember that you are dust, and unto dust you will return.'

Station 2

An opportunity to put the past behind you. On the table is a box of sand. You are invited to go forward and to write a confession in the sand: it can be a name, a word, a picture. When you have finished, go and stand in front of *(name)*, who will share with you these words of Jesus: 'Don't be afraid. I love you. You are forgiven. Go and sin no more.' *She/he* will then wipe away what you have written/drawn, so your words and pictures will remain private. Please do not approach the table until the sand has been smoothed.

Station 3

A reminder of your baptism. As you go forward you will be invited to kneel or stand in front of the font. You will receive a sprinkling of water and these words:

'Baptism welcomes you home and sends you out. Go and journey with God.'

Music to send folk back to their seat.

Words of forgiveness and hope:

Listen again to the words of Jesus:
'Don't be afraid.
I love you.
You are forgiven.
Go and sin no more.' **Amen**

Song

A closing blessing:

Bless us, God:
As we walk into the desert
send your angels to travel with us,
remind us that you are always near.

Bless us, God:
As we journey towards Easter
give us companions on the way,
both strangers and friends.

God of beauty and welcome,
Jesus who calls us,
Spirit of truth and challenge,
bless us *today/tonight* and always,
keep us in love.
Amen

Ruth Burgess and Sally Foster-Fulton

We don't like Ash Wednesday

Many of us, myself included, imagine ourselves superior to other people. We are smarter, we are stronger, we are wealthier, we are wiser, we are more faithful, we are simply more. This leads to a strong sense of individualism, but it also takes us into isolation: it makes us not need the other, and so we don't discover the gifts of the other. We don't like our common humanity, and so we don't like Ash Wednesday.

Many of us, especially me, don't like our mortality. We quickly turn past the obituaries in the newspaper; we find excuses not to attend the funeral of a neighbour; we are reluctant to visit someone who is in a hospice – especially if they are in their final hours. The death of someone may diminish us, it is true, but it also reminds us of our own death. We don't like to think of our mortality, and so we don't like Ash Wednesday.

Many of us, and I am one of the many, don't like God (it's OK, we can admit it). Oh, we hope God likes us, watches over us, cares for us and all the other things God is supposed to do for us. But this God who expects us to admit to all the screw-ups in our lives; this God who wants us to wear our faith on our forehead; this God who wants us to be Christ's emissaries in the broken places of our world; this God who wants us to break the bonds of oppression, to feed others from our pantries, to speak up for the voiceless, to pick up the fallen ... It's hard to like this God, and so we don't like Ash Wednesday.

We don't like Ash Wednesday. But when the ashes are placed on our forehead, something happens ... We are able to look around and see that we are as smudged, messy and broken as the person next to us, and that we are family not strangers. We are able to look at our frail, aging, wrinkling bodies and recognise we are not approaching the end of our journey, but coming up to a new path. We are able to look at God and see, not the One who has been shaped in our desires, dreams, fears, hopes, but the One who continues to transform us into people of justice, of hope, of freedom, of possibilities.

People of the kin-dom, we journey together during this season of Lent, and through all the seasons of our lives.

Thom M Shuman

Help us turn

Gracious God,
whose steadfast love never ceases:
by your hands we live
and to your hands we return when all our days are done.
Help us turn in our Lenten journey
from hopelessness to hope,
from self-concern to other-concern,
from empty conformity to radical discipleship.
As we bear these ashes on our face,
remind us that you have washed away the ashes on our souls.
Grant that the awareness of our mortality may lead us
not to fear, but to faith.
In our weakness teach us to look to you for strength,
in our failures to turn to you and find forgiveness,
and in our dying
to await the gift of everlasting life.

James Hart Brumm

Your mercy is so huge (Psalm 51)

Your mercy is so huge!
Wipe away all my sins.
Scrub away my guilt and
wash the sin out of me.
I know all about my sins; my guilt just doesn't go away.
You are the one I have really sinned against,
and you know every wrong thing I have done.
Whatever judgement you decide, I deserve,
for I have gotten it wrong since the day I was born. *(Psalm 51:1–5)*

We have come to you covered in sins, O God,
and you have answered us with forgiveness.
We are still smudged and dirty,
and you are still cleaning us up.
Please never stop, O God!
Please help us get it right!

Kyrie

You want truth from the inside out:
teach me, and fill me with your wisdom;
soak me clean in your laundry;
wash me whiter than snow;
fill my ears with joy and gladness;
fill my broken body with praises.
Don't look at my sins; just erase my guilt. *(Psalm 51:6–9)*

Now we stand before you free and forgiven,
but we know the work is far from done:
Lead us in the difficult transition from wrong to right,
from ugliness to beauty,
from crying to praising,
from death to life.

Please never stop, O God!
Please help us get it right!

Kyrie

God, give me a fresh, clean heart and a new, right spirit.
Don't throw me out with the trash.
Don't take your Holy Spirit away from me.
Fill me with the joy of knowing you have saved me,
and with your Spirit to direct me.
Then I will teach all sinners your Way
and they will come flocking back to you.
God, my saving God, keep me from destruction,
and I will sing out what you have done for me. *(Psalm 51:10–14)*

This is not the first time we have needed your fresh start,
nor will it be our last.
Keep the faith with us
and walk with us, step by step, on the Lenten journey.
Help us be your joy-filled people,
leading others into your love
and away from all the ways we would destroy ourselves.
Please never stop, O God!
Please help us get it right!

Open up my mouth, O God,
and I will let loose with your praise.
Meaningless ritual and empty gestures are nothing to you.
But when we are really humble, truly sorry,
then you will listen;
we know you will, O God. *(Psalm 51:15–17)*

Kyrie

Make the place where you are with us a delightful place, O God!
Rebuild the walls of your peace,
and you will get true worship from us;

you will get righteous worship from us;
we will pile up our offerings before you.
Please never stop, O God!
Please help us get it right!
Please make us strong as your Son's apostles,
even as we pray as your Son taught us:

Our Father ...

James Hart Brumm

Companions

I never know what to expect at an Ash Wednesday service, but over the years I have learned simply to wait for God to show up and take my breath away.

Last night I knew we wouldn't have a big crowd. We Presbyterians rarely do, and with the cold and snow yesterday, it would be fewer than normal. Those faithful folk who attend all such special services came; one couple brought their grandparents, with whom they share the joy of a new grandchild; a couple of old friends came because they saw the sign out in front; and, almost at the last moment, a father arrived with his six-year-old daughter. As they went to sit down, she whispered to him, 'I'm going to go sit with Thom,' and she did. I smiled at her and asked if she would be my assistant. With a big smile she announced, 'Dad, I'm Thom's assistant!'

At the point in the service for the placing of the ashes, I went around the circle, and came to her last, and with her wide eyes and wider hope, I was blessed to anoint her. And then, on the spur of the Spirit, I whispered to her, 'Will you put them on my forehead?' And with a wide smile and joyful spirit, she did. And I said a prayer to myself, hoping they would never come off. Later, during communion, I asked her to carry the loaf of bread around to folk, while I followed behind her with the cup. And by the end of the service, I was nearly breathless.

As I begin this sometimes lonely journey of discipleship during this season, I am reminded of all the companions I have had over the years. From Mrs Galt who took seriously my childhood yearning to sing, to Ms Helen who wrote poetry until her last day on earth; from the professor who was the only one who didn't laugh at my questions, to the security guard who stopped by my room on Christmas Eve to invite me to his house when I was staying on campus that holiday; from the friends I made on my sabbatical time all those years ago in Scotland, France and Ireland, and whom I may never see again, to those 'virtual' friends who encourage me in ways they will never know – I have been surrounded by an incredible cloud of witnesses.

But it is the children I remember most. The little girl at the church Bonnie and I attended when we first got married who called me 'Magic Man' because I would pull a coin out of her ear; my nieces and nephews who have grown up into people who continue to amaze me; John, Margaret, Helen and Francis who challenged me with their questions and inspire me with the lives they lead as adults; the preschoolers who will be waiting in a couple of hours for Dusty the Church Dog and me to come read to them and to feed Dusty carrots and broccoli.

By God's goodness, so many of my companions on this journey have been children, and by God's grace, I hope I will continue to be blessed.

Thom M Shuman

Resources for Lent: Common Lectionary Year A

Collects for Lent

First Sunday in Lent (Matthew 4:1–11)

O Christ, who entered into the lonely desert,
and who, facing hunger, danger and temptation,
did not turn aside
but affirmed the way of self-giving love,
strengthen us to resist the false attraction of easy answers,
magic fixes,
abuses of power,
and the delusion that there is any way apart from justice
in which God's justice can be done.

Second Sunday in Lent (John 3:1–17)

O Christ, as you were lifted up upon the cross,
exposed for all the world to see, and sneer, and abandon,
give us courage not to abandon those also exposed
by poverty, unemployment or stigma
to the risk of unprotected living,
and faith to believe that even we
may be born again
in the Spirit of love.

Third Sunday in Lent (John 4:5–42)

O Christ, as you spoke with the woman at the well
and drank from her cup
to the scandal of your disciples,
because of her indignity,
grant that we who are habitually scandalised
by everyone except ourselves,
may learn from you to refrain from judgement,
to accord respect to all God's children,
and so be privileged to hear the witness
of those the world treats with indignity.

Fourth Sunday in Lent (John 9:1–41)

O Christ our enlightener,
once and for all,
you broke the link between suffering and punishment,
erased the line between deserving and undeserving
and invited the unseeing to open their eyes to the truth about themselves.
Doing this, you revealed yourself,
became vulnerable.
Preserve us from the defendedness that makes us vicious,
give us insight to see the structures of injustice by which we profit,
and grace to cherish all people in our vulnerability,
knowing that we all live within your love.

Fifth Sunday in Lent (John 11:1–45)

O Christ, lover and friend,
who felt the desolation of death
and the fear of abandonment
and yet practised 'yes' in the midst of each despairing 'no',
may we, who also recognise the shape of desolation
and weep,
practise 'no' in the midst of each complicit 'yes'.
No to profiteering and exploitation,
no to indifference and abuse,
no for the sake of the resurrection yes.

Kathy Galloway

I am long and very slithery (Genesis 2 and 3)

This is probably best spoken by a voice offstage – but if you want a focus, drape a stuffed snake over a branch – centre stage.

Hello.

Let me introduce myself.

I am long and very sssslithery.

I appear in many guissssses and in lots of storiessssss.

Nobody seems to like me and I always get a very bad pressss.

Have you guessssed which animal I am?

Yesssss, that'ssss right – I'm a sssssnake.

And if you're really clever you've guessssed which Bible ssssstory we're going to think about this morning.

It's in the book of Genesissss.

Yesssss, right again, it's the story about me and Adam and Eve in the garden, the ssssumptuous Garden of Eden.

You remember the story? God had planted a garden in Eden.

A beautiful garden with a huge orchard in the middle full of fruit treesssss.

And God had formed a man out of the dust. And God had formed birds and animals that the man named.

The man named me sssnake and the teller of this story paid me a great compliment – he said I was the most devioussss, cunning creature that God had ever made – impressssive, eh?

And God had told the man he was to look after the garden, and that he could eat the fruit of nearly every tree in the garden. And God showed the man two sssspecial trees in the middle of the garden. They were beautiful treesssss – ssssssuperb ssspecimensssss. God called one tree the tree that givesss life. The other tree God called the tree that givessss knowledge of good and evil. And God told the man not to eat fruit from the tree that givesss knowledge of good and evil, for if he did eat that fruit he would die.

And you remember that God had made a woman out of one of the man'sss bonesss and they both now lived in the garden – naked like all the rest of ussss.

I loved living in the garden. I could move sssilently from tree to tree and I could eavesssdrop on what everyone was sssaying. There wassss a lot of talk about food. There was so much of it. And every fruit had a different taste and they were all deli-cioussss.

The woman interesssted me. Like me, she asked quessstionsss. She was curioussss. I teasssed her one day.

I said: 'Woman, did God really tell you that you ssshouldn't eat any fruit in thisss garden?'

She smiled, and replied, 'We can eat all the fruit we like in this garden – and the fruit is delicious – but God has told us that we mustn't eat the fruit from the tree in the middle of the garden – the tree that gives knowledge of good and evil. God said if we eat fruit from that tree we shall die.'

I said, 'That'sss not true you know – you won't die – but if you eat that fruit you will know things that you never knew before – you will be like God – you will know what issss good and what issss evil.'

The woman walked to the middle of the garden and she looked at the two trees. I had made her more curioussss. The tree of life was beautiful. God had said she could eat from that one. And the tree that gave knowledge of good and evil looked even more beautiful. Itsss fruit looked ssssuperb. The woman thought that it would be wonderful to be wise. She stood at the foot of the tree and I sssslitherd up the tree trunk and looped my body around a branch full of fruit. The woman hesitated – was I right ... was God right? The fruit looked delicious.

The woman stretched out her hand, and picked some of the fruit and she ate it. And then she called her husband and gave him some of the fruit, and he ate some too. They were still alive. I wasss right. They didn't die.

But then sssomething strange happened. The man and the woman went and gathered leaves and fastened them together and hung them around themselves. The woman refused to talk to me again so I have no idea what that wassss about.

I think about the other tree sometimes – the tree of life – and I often wonder what would have happened if the woman had not listened to me – but she did – she made her choice – and choices alwaysss have consequencesssss – and you probably remember the rest of the story. Enough to say that I'll always ssslither around on my belly, and me and my children will always keep out of the way of humanssss – they don't like us very much – curioussss – I wonder why.

Ruth Burgess, Spill the Beans

The unexpected move (Genesis 12:1–9)

It's hard to be uprooted at my age.
'Pack your bags,' he said.
'Why, where are we going?'
'I don't know,' he replied. 'Just pack your bags.'
Well, I know women must obey their husbands but this was too much.
'How long are we going for?' I asked.
'What do you mean we're moving?'
I thought we had settled here. All our family are here.
I know many of the people around us are nomadic
but I thought we were different.
We've made our money and have settled down.

Why should we get up and move on at this time in our lives?
I'm sixty-six and Abram seventy-five.
And what did he mean that God told him to? Who is this God?
Our gods belong here in this place.
But not this one, apparently.

He has told Abram that
he is going to take him to a land that he will show him
and give that land to our descendants.
Our descendants!
At our age!
We gave up hope of having children long ago.
What's the use of having land if we have no sons to pass it on to?

I have no desire to move.
But as his wife I have no choice.
It will not be easy.
We have many possessions and animals.
At least we have servants, too.
They will do the packing and the carrying.
But I don't want to leave what has been my home for so long.
I don't know what the future will hold for us.
And yet, I feel confident that this God who has told Abram to go
will be with us.

Margaret Roe

Abram and Sarai (Genesis 12)

I went on a long journey a few weeks ago. I was going to see a friend. I did my packing first. Some clothes, a book to read, a towel and a toothbrush, and my teddy bear. And I took some sandwiches and coffee for the journey.

Have you been on a journey?

Can you remember what you packed to take with you?

I've moved house a few times. That takes lots of packing. It needs a van to move the furniture and it means saying goodbye to your friends. When you get to your new place it means making lots of new friends.

Has anyone ever moved?

What do you remember about it?

Abram and Sarai were two people in the Bible who did lots of moving. When they moved they took lots of things and people with them. They took sheep and goats and cattle. They took people to look after the animals. And they carried pots and pans and food and water and clothes and tent-poles and tents.

One day God said to Abram: 'I want you to leave your home and travel to a new land that I will show you.' Abram could have said no to God. He could have said: 'I'm an old man – I don't want to travel any more. I want to stay at home.' But Abram didn't say no, he said yes. And when people say yes to God, all sorts of things can happen, and they did.

Abram was 75 years old and his wife Sarai was not much younger when they started off on their adventure. Their nephew, who was called Lot, went with them. Abram and Sarai and their family and servants packed up their clothes and furniture, filled up the water bottles, rounded up all the animals, packed up the tents, said goodbye to some of their family who were staying behind, said goodbye to their friends and set off on their journey with God.

Ruth Burgess, Spill the Beans

Nicodemus' song (John 3)

(Tune: 'Samuel')

Dark were the city streets;
the night watch on patrol
had passed the alleyway, down which a figure stole.
A seeker on a quest was bound;
what would this night be lost or found?

Responding to his knock,
the door was opened wide.
Compelled by all he'd seen and heard, he stepped inside.
A strict observer of the Law
here was a truth he must explore.

Sincere in his respect
the conversation flows
and deepens, as awareness of Christ's Kingdom grows.
A Kingdom which is now and here:
spirituality made clear.

He wonders at the words
and tries to understand.
New and eternal life in Christ go hand in hand,
who shows the magnitude of grace
and holds the world in Love's embrace.

The gift of Christ today
is open unto all;
a life lived out in love, the answer to his call.
And those who come to Christ by night
become the children of the light.

Avis Palmer

Whoosh! Gurgle! Splossshhh! (Exodus 17)

This is a story from long ago when Moses was leading his people away from Egypt to a new home in a better land.

They had been walking through the desert for a long time and there was no water. Not a drip drop.

'I'm thirsty!' someone said.

'Me too!' shouted another.

'Give us some water, Moses!'

Soon everyone was saying it – a whole big crowd of hot, thirsty, grumpy people.

'Give us some water! Give us some water!'

Moses started feeling very hot and grumpy too.

What was he supposed to do to get water for all his friends in the middle of a desert?

But they kept shouting, 'Give us some water! Give us some water! And tell us, is God still here with us or has God gone away and left us!'

So Moses complained to God, 'What am I supposed to do, God? What am I supposed to do for all these hot, thirsty, grumpy people? They want me to give them water but what can I do about it? And are you still with us, God? ... Hellloooo? Are you still with us, or have you gone away and left us?'

Well, the people were grumpy and Moses was grumpy, but God didn't get grumpy. The people thought God might have gone away and Moses thought God might have gone away, but God hadn't gone away and left them.

God listened to all the hot, thirsty, grumpy people and he loved them very much; so he said to Moses, 'Follow me to that big rock over there. Hit the rock with your stick!'

So Moses went to the big rock and hit it with his stick.

WHOOSH! GURGLE! SPLOSSSHHH!

Water came pouring out and everyone had enough to drink.

Jo Love

I do not judge as you judge (1 Samuel 16)

God told Samuel the prophet that one of Jesse's sons would be the next King of Israel.

So Samuel went to see Jesse.

One by one, Jesse called each of his sons before Samuel.

First his eldest son.

Samuel thought: *This boy is tall and strong. People would look up to him.*

But God said to Samuel, 'No, this is not the one I choose.'

The second son was very honest and clever.

Samuel thought: *This man would rule justly.*

But God said to Samuel, 'No, this is not the one I choose.'

The third son was holy. He prayed every day.

Samuel thought: *Perhaps this is the man whom God has chosen.*

But God said to Samuel, 'No, this is not the one I choose.'

Jesse's fourth son was a warrior: he could have led Israel into battle; another son was polite and would have made a good diplomat; another managed people wisely; but each time God said to Samuel, 'No, this is not the one I choose.'

Samuel said to Jesse, 'Haven't you any more sons?'

Jesse answered him: 'Well, there is still my youngest son, David, but he's just a boy. He's only old enough to look after the sheep.'

So David was sent for.

He was healthy and good-looking, and he had a twinkle in his eye.

And God said to Samuel, 'This is the one: make him king.'

And God said to Samuel, 'You see I do not judge as you judge. I am not interested in how strong people look, or how sensible or holy they seem to be. I look at what people are like inside. I look at what people value. I look at who they are and who they can become.'

And Samuel took the horn of oil and anointed David, and God's Spirit was with David from that day on.

Ruth Burgess

Dem bones, dem bones (Ezekiel 37)

Andy: *(singing)* Dem bones, dem bones gonna walk aroun'. Dem bones, dem bones gonna walk aroun'. Dem bones, dem bones gonna walk aroun'. I hear the word of the Lord! ...

Ada: Andy, what's that terrible racket you're making?

Andy: I'm singing!

Ada: Is that what you call it? It sounded like the dog was choking.

Andy: Naw, Ada, I am singing that old spiritual we learned years ago at the Sunday Club. Dem bones, dem bones gonna walk aroun'. Dem bones, dem bones gonna walk aroun'. Dem bones, dem bones gonna walk aroun'. I hear the word of the Lord!

Ada: Why are you singing *that* song? Why not 'Jesus loves me'? Or 'Give me oil in my lamp'? Or something that everyone knows and could join in?

Andy: Well, Ada, it's because I was thinking about the Bible reading from today that came from the book of Ezekiel. The prophet is in a valley full of dry bones.

Ada: What do you mean he was in a valley of dry bones? Was he in an old graveyard or at some abattoir?

Andy: What's an abattoir?

Ada: It's a place where meat is processed.

Andy: Oh, I don't think they had been invented yet, Ada, so I guess Ezekiel must have been in an old cemetery or something.

Ada: It sounds pretty gruesome to me. You wouldn't find me dead in a place like that!

Andy: Well, Ada, if you were in a cemetery you probably would be dead.

Ada: Okay, Andy, don't get smart with me. The question is, what was Ezekiel doing in a cemetery?

Andy: *(picks up a Bible)* It says here that God led him out into the valley and told him to prophesy.

Ada: Prophesy, you say. Do you know what that means, Andy?

Andy: I remember our minister telling us it was someone speaking on behalf of God to the people of God, or letting someone else know that God is onto them.

Ada: Very good, Andy, couldn't have put it better myself. But what is God going to do with a pile of dry bones?

Andy: Bring them to life, it says here. He is going to put flesh on the bones, breathe God's Spirit into them, and bring them to life.

Ada: Och, Andy, you have to be joking – let me read that. *(Takes Bible from Andy and begins reading and mumbling aloud)* … Oh right, so it does.

Andy: That's amazing, isn't it? A bit weird, like, but amazing. Do you think

God could do that today? Nip down the cemetery, dig up some bones, put some flesh on them, breathe life into them, and bring my mammy and ma granny back to life?

Ada: Er … no, Andy, I don't think that's what's intended here. It is a metaphor, not a literal story.

Andy: A metaphor? Is that like a made-up story?

Ada: Not quite, Andy, it portrays the meaning of something in an exaggerated sense. The prophet is telling us about the things God can do, and he can breathe life into anything, even a pile of dry bones if he wanted to.

Andy: Do you think he could breathe life into this lot here *(pointing to the congregation)*?

Ada: Oh, I am sure that he could. God can do anything he wants, even bring life where death and decay sets in.

Andy: Oh, look … I think I can see God breathing life into wee Mrs McGlumpher over there, and Big Bob in the corner there, and wee Nellie over there!

Ada: Aye, when our hopes are dashed, and the world seems to have gone to pot, God can bring about change, life and renewal. That's what Ezekiel wanted for the people of Israel; and that's what God can still do for the people of *(your location)* – even today.

Andy: Well, Ada, are you ready to join in my wee song now?

Ada: Okay, Andy, let's go for it.

Both: Dem bones, dem bones gonna walk aroun'. Dem bones, dem bones gonna walk aroun'. Dem bones, dem bones gonna walk aroun'. I hear the word of the Lord! …

John Murning, Spill the Beans

Resources for Lent:
Common Lectionary Year B

I saw a dove (Mark 1:9–15)

Child: Hey, Mum, you'll never believe what I've just seen.

Mum: Go on, surprise me.

Child: I saw a dove descending from heaven!

Mum: There is nothing unusual in that. Doves are meant to fly.

Child: But this was a talking dove!

Mum: What do you mean a talking dove? Doves don't talk, they just make cooing noises!

Child: But, Mum, this dove *did* talk. It said: 'You are my Son, whom I love. With you I am well- pleased.'

Mum: But that doesn't make sense. Doves don't fly around talking to people. Who else was there?

Child: Well, there was a man in the river, dressed up in a camel-hair swimsuit. And he was with another man called Jesus. And the man in the camel-hair swimsuit ducked the man called Jesus under the water, and when he came out the water, the dove appeared and it spoke to Jesus, who was trying to catch his breath after being ducked under the water.

Mum: What have I told you about playing down at the river? It's too dangerous for children of your age – you could have fallen in and been carried away by the current. You could have drowned!

Child: But, Mum, the talking dove! We could make a fortune if we had a talking dove. It would be an end to all our poverty. We could take it to the market and charge people to hear our amazing talking dove.

Mum: Away and don't be daft. Whoever heard of such a thing as a talking dove anyway. Away and get your homework done and put all this nonsense out of your head.

(Pause)

Child: But, Mum, suppose that dove was the voice of God speaking to Jesus. What would that mean for all of us?

Mum: That would mean all the difference in the world then. In fact, it makes a lot more sense than a talking dove.

Spill the Beans

Baptism

Already up to your middle,
the pressure on the back of your head gets harder
until there is nothing for it
but to let yourself be pushed under.

The abrupt cold shocks you,
disorientates you.
Your deep breath of preparation
gets choked up on entry.

You can see only sinister suggestions
of things you would rather not know.
That leaden hand
keeps you breathlessly under.

The pressure relents.
You emerge dazzled,
the water stinging your eyes.
You struggle not to stumble.

You scrape back
your tangle of hair and the weeds
and try to find your 'all in a day's work' face.
But above, something catches your eye.

You look up,
wiping the last drops from your eyes.
It's coming down,
whatever it is.

You are tingling, energised but relaxed.
This is more than a cold-water shock.
You can think only one word:
peace.

You hear a voice
somehow attached to it,
somehow coming down,
somehow directed at you.

'You belong to me.
I'm proud of you.'

Katherine Fox

I wonder (Mark 1:9–15)

Here's a story about something Jesus really wanted to do. It was when he grew up, but before he was famous. It was before he had made any sick people better, before he had told any amazing stories, before he did any miracles, before lots of people got to know him.

Jesus wanted to go away by himself for a while. He wanted to be alone.

I wonder why he wanted to be alone.

I wonder where he could go to be alone.

He decided to go for a long walk out into the desert.

I wonder what it was like to be in the desert.

I wonder what Jesus did while he was alone there.

Later, lots of people got to know Jesus and he became quite famous for his stories and his miracles.

I wonder if he still liked to get away by himself and be alone sometimes.

I wonder what's good about us being by ourselves sometimes too.

Jo Love, Spill the Beans

I put my trust (Psalm 25)

In you, Lord my God,
I put my trust.
I trust in you;
do not let me be put to shame,
nor let my enemies triumph over me.
No one who hopes in you
will ever be put to shame,
but shame will come on those
who are treacherous without cause.
Show me your ways, Lord,
teach me your paths. *(Psalm 25:1–4)*

We are taking our first Lenten steps, O God,
remembering how you sent Noah and his family
away from the safety of the ark,
remembering how you stayed with Jesus
to face the dangers of the desert.
We are taking our first steps, in faith and in trust.
Show us your ways, O Lord;
teach us your paths.

Silence

We are taking our first steps, Creator God,
knowing we are surrounded by dangers,
remembering many of them are of our own making.
We pray for this world, and for all the people in it.
Make us good stewards of all that you have given us:
land, water, sky, plants, creatures and people.
Be with those in places of conflict or danger this day …
Be with those who lay down their lives for others …
Be with those who lead us …
Show us your ways, O Lord;
teach us your paths.

Silence

We are taking our first steps, Nurturing God,
knowing many people are in trouble,
remembering we are called to bring them your care.
We pray for all those who are alone,
all those who are imprisoned,
and all those who are ill or infirm …
Show us your ways, O Lord;
teach us your paths.

Silence

We are taking our first steps, Shepherding God,
knowing we are called to be the body of Christ,
remembering we are to be the light
showing your path to the world.
We pray for your holy Church …
Show us your ways, O Lord;
teach us your paths.

Silence

We are taking our first Lenten steps, O God.
Guide me in your truth and teach me,
for you are God my Saviour,
and my hope is in you all day long.
Remember, Lord, your great mercy and love,
for they are from of old.
Do not remember the sins of my youth
and my rebellious ways;
according to your love remember me,
for you, Lord, are good.

Good and upright is the Lord:
instructing sinners in God's ways,
guiding the humble in what is right
and teaching them God's way.
All the ways of the Lord are loving and faithful
toward those who keep the demands of his covenant. *(Psalm 25:5–10)*
Hear these and all our prayers, great God,

in the name of Christ, in whose footsteps we follow.
Amen

James Hart Brumm

We bring to God

As we contemplate the luxury
of wilderness,
as we crave the beauty of peace,
as we long for the tranquility
of space carved out
in which to meet the living God,
we bring to God
those whose days seem endless,
whose lives seem too full of quiet,
who long for the clamour and noise
of the loved ones they have lost,
and for tasks to fill up their days.

We bring to God
those filled with bitterness and resentment
at brutality and injustice,
those whom God welcomes and longs
to cradle in love.

As we contemplate Lenten austerity
we bring to God
those who experience real poverty and need,
day after day after day …

And we know that the Christ of the wilderness
hangs back, slowing his step
so that he can walk alongside all
who are bowed down
with the heavy burden
that life has become.

The Christ of the wilderness
offers food for the journey,
healing for the road,
strength for the weary,
comfort for the sorrowing,
grace, peace and love.
Thanks be to God. Amen

Liz Crumlish, Spill the Beans

We come to you with wonder and awe (Psalm 22:23–31)

A: We praise you, O God!
We glorify you!
We come to you with wonder and awe,
knowing you will hear our prayers.

B: God who does not turn away from the afflicted,
who always hears our cries,
we pray for those who are in special need this day:
for those who are in prison or alone,
for those who are ill or infirm,
for those who mourn;
and we give thanks for those
who have found your healing in their lives.

Silence

C: God who gathers us into the great congregation
and around whose table we eat and are satisfied,
as we seek you and lead others to you,
we pray for your holy Church:
for this congregation gathered here,
for sisters and brothers in our community,
for your Church around the world,
for all whose lives proclaim your praise.

Silence

D: God who rules over all the nations,
who cares for us even when we do not recognise you,
we pray for this world, where you call us to be stewards:
We pray for your help in caring for creation.
We pray for your protection over those in conflict or danger this day.
We pray for your strength for those who lay down their lives
to protect brothers, sisters and neighbours.
We pray for your wisdom for the leaders of nations, cities and towns.

Silence

A: All who sleep in the earth,
all who become dust
will bow down before you,
and I will live for you.
Posterity will serve you.
Future generations will be told about you.
People not yet born will be saved by you.
We pray with confidence,
knowing that you have already done it.

James Hart Brumm

For generations (John 2:13–22)

My family have had a stall in this temple for generations. My father, and his father before him, and his before that, all ran this stall selling the best-quality doves and sheep for sacrifice. We personally source the animals from local farmers, and each one is meticulously inspected and well-cared-for until we sell it on to one of the pilgrims. This stall is not just a job to me: it's a way of life, a tradition and an expression of my religious devotion and duty to ensure that animals offered to God are the very best available. There are others out to make a quick denarius or two, but I'm not one of them!

There are many pilgrims who think we rip them off. However, we have to cover all our costs. There is the rental of the stall site, taxes on every animal we sell and the host of certificates required for trading. Good animals do not come cheaply, and the profits we make help my family to live, but certainly not in any form of luxury.

Today something happened that in all my years of trading in the holy temple I have never witnessed before – it was like a wild mob was running riot through the temple. At first we thought it was some foreign insurgents daring to desecrate this holy place.

However, it turned out that it was one of our own who was causing all the trouble. His name is Jesus of Nazareth. He has been making quite a name for himself as a teacher and a healer, and a number of people have already begun to proclaim him as the Messiah. In fact, the other day he arrived in the city on top of a donkey and people were waving palm branches in the air and throwing down their coats and hailing him as a king.

Yet what kind of king would overturn the tables of legitimate businessmen going about their godly business? What kind of king would set animals free and take up a whip and chase people out of the temple? What kind of king would act in such a violent, ungodly way? What this Jesus did today was beyond the pale!

Jesus said that we were turning God's holy house into a den of thieves and robbers – but we were not the ones acting violently. We were the ones going about our legitimate godly business, and not wrecking stalls and chasing people with whips. This is no gentle, meek and mild king. This is a dangerous and violent individual determined to undermine the religious authorities and the good, honest working people of Jerusalem.

The religious authorities dealt quickly with the incident, but I was frightened and upset by this personal attack, and I hope they ban him from all future temple events and let us get on with our own godly business. However, I fear this is not the end of the story or the last we will hear of this Jesus of Nazareth.

Spill the Beans

Mr Nice Guy (John 2:13–17)

Mr Nice Guy. Some people think Jesus is Mr Nice Guy. I wonder what you think?

Here's a story about Jesus:

He was going to the biggest church he knew, in the biggest city he knew. When people went to that big church in those days, they had to buy an animal, maybe a sheep or a dove, and they gave the animal to God as a way of saying, 'Thank you, God', or 'Sorry, God', or 'Help me, God'.

But lots of people had no money to buy anything to give God. It wasn't fair. Surely God listened to people saying thank you or sorry or please help me, even if they had nothing to give God when they prayed.

Jesus walked into the big church and saw all the rich people selling their animals and making money. And he saw all the poor people feeling sad, thinking God wouldn't listen to their prayers. So Jesus decided to do something about it.

He chased the animals out and tipped the plates of money on the floor! 'Get out of here!' he shouted. 'This is a place for everyone to pray – it's not for shopping!'

I wonder why Jesus did that.

I wonder what he was thinking.

I wonder what you think about Jesus not being Mr Nice Guy.

Jo Love, Spill the Beans

What kind of Saviour?

Gentle, meek, mild, insipid.
What kind of Saviour is that?
Wishy-washy, ineffective.
Not someone we'd respect.

So why is it shocking to discover that Jesus is a man of passion,
seized with righteous anger,
wielding a whip,
driving out those who drive out others,
and make God's house exclusive?

Why should we be surprised that Jesus doesn't just speak out
but takes action to ensure that all people,
everywhere, have access to the love of God?
And that, following this feisty man
means that we too must be people of action?

Spill the Beans

God of passion

God of passion, we give you thanks today
for all those who are passionate about your kingdom,
for those who speak up to ensure that all your children
are treated with fairness and compassion.

We give you thanks
for those who work to ensure that none are excluded
because of race or gender or sexual orientation,
for those who work hard to include the poor and the marginalised,
the unloved and the unwanted.
We give you thanks for all those who embody your love –
a love that knows no bounds.

As we give you thanks for passion and love,
help us to embrace those qualities in ourselves.

Starting with this place and with these people,
may we reach out to one another.
May we be known as a welcoming worshipping community
where there is always room for more
and where the love of God is freely shared
with all who come.
In the name of God who bids all welcome.
Amen

Liz Crumlish, Spill the Beans

Your glory fills the heavens (Psalm 19)

God, your glory fills the heavens
and all that you have made bears your mark.
We pray for this creation:
we ask forgiveness for the ways in which we have disfigured it;
we pray for those who cannot enjoy
the warm sun or the cool night:
those who are imprisoned or alone …
those who are ill or infirm …
those who mourn …
Use all of us, our hearts, our hands,
to bring your wondrous power into their lives.
Let us glorify you, O God.
Let your hymn resound in our lives.

Silence

God, your perfect law protects and revives us
and your way enlightens and enlivens us.
We pray for all the peoples of this world,
people hungry for warmth and shelter, order and safety …
women and men who lay down their lives to keep their neighbours safe …
and those who lead our nations, cities and towns …
Help us unearth the treasure of justice and equality
and bring it to all the world.

Let us glorify you, O God.
Let your hymn resound in our lives.

Silence

God, who brings the true sweetness,
the true riches of life to those who serve you,
who gathers, protects and preserves us,
we pray for your holy Church …
Keep us blameless and innocent.
Cleanse our faults,
increase our faith,
inspire our work and witness in your name.
Let us glorify you, O God.
Let your hymn resound in our lives.

Silence

Hear these and all our prayers, great God.
Let the words of our mouths
and the meditations of our hearts
be acceptable to you, O Lord,
our Rock and Redeemer.

James Hart Brumm

Lifted up (John 3:14–21)

Andy: Ada, what do you think 'lifted up' means?

Ada: Well, Andy, lifted up is usually what I do after you all the time. I lift up the socks you leave lying on the bedroom floor. I lift up the teacups that I find all over the house. I lift up –

Andy: I don't mean that kind of lifted up. I mean people getting lifted.

Ada: Oh, that's what the polis used to do on a Saturday night to you before you found Jesus.

Andy: Naw. It's in the Bible here! It talks about Moses lifting up a snake and of Jesus getting lifted up.

Ada: Oh, that Moses must have been awful brave to lift up a snake. I am awfy feart of snakes and creepy-crawlies.

Andy: Now, Ada, I am no worried about your phobias. I need to know what it means for Jesus tae be lifted up.

Ada: Well, maybe it means like that time when Airdrie won the Alba Cup and they lifted up Paul Lovering and carried him about the park with the trophy *(choose your own team or famous moment)*. Maybe Simon Peter and Andrew put him up on their shoulders and carried him around the town.

Andy: Eh, I don't think that football had been invented then, Ada, so it might no have been like that!

Ada: Well, maybe he was trying to get a vantage point to talk to all the crowds who were following him, so they lifted him up to stand on some shed or something.

Andy: No, I don't think it means that either, for it says that he must be lifted up that everyone who believes in him may have eternal life.

Ada: Is this meant to be some cryptic crossword clue?

Andy: No, it's the words from the Bible.

Ada: Well, it sounds like it must be really important. Maybe it means the cross. You know, when Jesus was nailed and lifted up on the cross to die for our sins.

Andy: Ah, now that makes sense. We know that he died on the cross for you and me, Ada. To be lifted up must mean that he shows everyone just how much God loves them, for everyone can see the cross on Calvary hill and know that God really cares for them because he died that we might all have life.

Ada: Aye, Jesus is no some celebrity footballer, he is God's own dear son. 'For God so loved the world that he gave his one and only Son, that whoever believes in him shall not perish but have eternal life.'

Andy: My your awfy good at memorising your Bible. That comes from John 3 verse 16, the most famous verse in the Bible.

Ada: Well, your doing no bad yourself at finding out about Jesus. I wonder if the folk in our congregation here read their Bibles as much as you do these days.

Andy: *(turning to the congregation)* Well, do you?

John Murning, Spill the Beans

We come to you (Psalm 107:1–3,17–22)

We come to you in prayer, O God.
We know your steadfast love endures forever.
We pray for a world sick through our sinful ways,
with an environment that is out of balance,
with economies that are out of balance,
with nations whose policies are out of balance.
We pray to you: come save us.
We pray for people in places of conflict and danger this day …
for those who give their lives to keep their families, friends,
and neighbours safe …
and for our leaders …

Silence

We come to you in prayer, O God.
We know your steadfast love endures forever.
We pray for a people who are sick and afflicted
through our sinful ways,
sick and afflicted through broken relationships,
sick and afflicted because of poverty and hunger,
sick and afflicted because of bodies distressed and near death.
We pray to you: come heal us.
We pray for those who are imprisoned or alone today …
for those who are ill or infirm …
and for those who mourn …

Silence

We come to you in prayer, O God.
We know your steadfast love endures forever.
We pray for your Church,
sent to heal and deliver our world
but beset by fears,
bogged down by petty problems,
broken by lavish egos.
We pray to you: come gather us at your table.
We pray for this congregation gathered here …

Silence

We come to you in prayer, O God.
We thank you for your steadfast love
and your wonderful works.
Remake our lives as thanksgiving sacrifices.
Send us forth to tell of your deeds with songs of joy.
Hear these and all our prayers,
in the name of your Son, Jesus Christ,
whom you sent to save us.

James Hart Brumm

This is the truth (John 12:20–33)

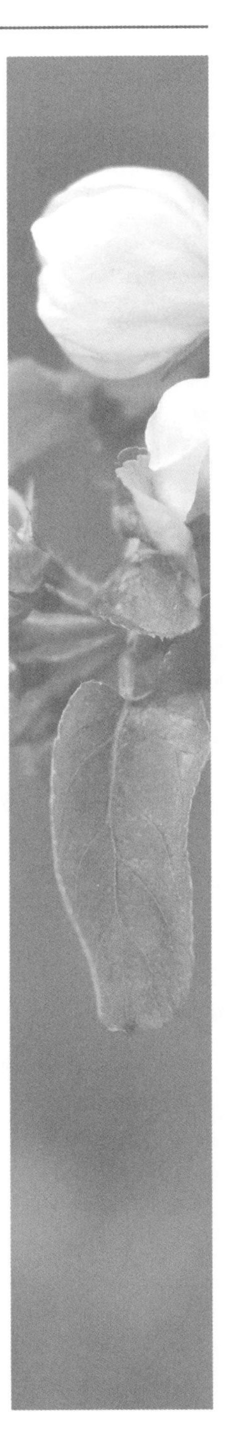

This is the truth.

A grain of wheat
remains a single grain
unless it is dropped into the earth
and dies.

In the earth
its death
brings forth new life.

If you love your life
you'll lose it.

But if loving me
is more important to you
than loving your life in this world,
you will always be with me,
always.

Follow me
love me
serve me
love your neighbours.

Do this and God will honour you,
keep you
bless you
always.

Ruth Burgess

You show us how to let go (John 12:20–33)

You show us how to let go
of all that holds us back,
of all that limits us,
of all that shames us.
Lord of the impossible,
we thank you for your challenge.

You leave us with no choice
but to seize life,
to share in its pleasures,
to not worry too much.
Lord of the impossible,
we thank you for your challenge.

You share with us that to do this,
to be your disciples,
we cannot continue on the way
we have always travelled,
leading the lives we have always led.
We need to let go.
Lord of the impossible,
we thank you for your challenge.

You challenge us all
to live a new life,
to love in new ways,
to care for your world.
Lord of the impossible,
we thank you for your challenge.

God of our lives
help us
through your grace;

bury us in your love
so that we may begin to live life
more abundantly.
Lord of the impossible,
we thank you for your challenge.

Spill the Beans

We who gather (Psalm 119:9–16)

How can those who are young keep their way pure?
By living according to your word.
I seek you with all my heart;
do not let me stray from your commands.
I have hidden your word in my heart
that I might not sin against you.
Praise be to you, Lord;
teach me your decrees.
With my lips I recount all the laws that come from your mouth.
I rejoice in following your statutes
as one rejoices in great riches.
I meditate on your precepts
and consider your ways.
I delight in your decrees;
I will not neglect your word. *(Psalm 119:9–16)*

**We who are young,
we who are old,
we who are rich,
we who are poor,
we who gather from every way and walk of life,
seeking you with our whole hearts,
trying to guard our lives according to your Word,
come to you in prayer.**

The worship leader or congregation may offer up particular thanksgivings and concerns, each followed by a time of silent prayer.

We who seek you with our whole heart
offer you our prayers,
in the name of Christ, your Son, our Saviour,
whose life was laid down that all our lives might rise.

James Hart Brumm

Resources for Lent:
Common Lectionary Year C

In the desert (Luke 4:1–13)

Jesus had been in the desert for 40 days. The desert in Israel is rocky, not sandy. Jesus had been there six weeks – that's ages. He was hungry and thirsty and tired, and who should appear round a rock but the devil himself.

Jesus and the devil eyed each other up and down – they were ready, ready for a good old row.

'Morning, Jesus,' said the devil.

'Morning, Satan,' said Jesus (cos that was the devil's name).

'Dare you!' said the devil.

'Pardon?' said Jesus.

'Dare you,' said the devil. 'Dare you to pick up a stone and turn it into bread.'

Jesus was quick with a reply: 'No way,' he said. 'You need more than bread to live on. I may be hungry but I'm not going to do that.'

They stared at each other. Then the devil tried again.

'Let's go for a walk up the mountain,' he said.

They stood on the mountaintop and looked over the edge.

'Dare you!' said the devil.

'Dare me what, Satan?' said Jesus.

'Dare you to say that there's no God and that I, Satan, am in charge of the world.'

'Pardon?' said Jesus.

'Dare you,' said Satan. 'And if you admit that I'm in charge of the world, I'll give it to you to rule over.'

Jesus laughed. 'No deal, Satan,' he said. 'God's in charge, not you, and you know that's true.'

Satan was cross – very cross. He'd tried twice to get Jesus to come in with him and Jesus was having none of it. OK, thought Satan, one last try. Third time lucky.

'Let's go to Jerusalem,' he said to Jesus.

So off they went. Jerusalem is a huge city and the devil took Jesus right to the top of a high tower on a building called the Temple. They looked down; the people in the city looked tiny from where they stood.

'Dare you to jump off!' said the devil. 'Go on! If God's looking after you he'll send his angels to catch you – you'll be fine. Everyone will be really impressed. Go on, jump. I'll give you a push if you like.'

'No,' said Jesus. 'I trust God to look after me. I don't have to test him to know that he cares about me. No, Satan, you can jump if you like but I'm not going to.'

The devil had had enough. Although Jesus was tired and hungry he still knew that God loved him. There seemed to be no way that Jesus would come over to the devil's side. So the devil went away. He might come back later and try again, but for now he was beat.

Ruth Burgess, Spill the Beans

Forty days

Forty days. Can you count? You can use your fingers to help. Ready?

Let's go: 1, 2, 3, 4, 5, 6, 7, 8, 9, 10.

Okay, that was good. Can you do 11 to 20? Might need to use your fingers and thumbs twice, maybe your toes. Ready?

Let's go: 11, 12, 13, 14, 15, 16, 17, 18, 19, 20. Okay. Good.

Now let's think about a day.

What time do you usually get up?

Have breakfast? Go to school? Etc.

Keep going through a typical day.

End with this last question:

How long do you sleep for most nights?

A day is a long time.

Let's count now right through from 1 to 20. Ready?

Let's go: 1, 2, 3, 4, 5, 6, 7, 8, 9, 10, 11, 12, 13, 14, 15, 16, 17, 18, 19, 20. Brilliant!

There's a story in the Bible about Jesus being on his own in the desert for 40 days. The desert is a lonely place: no people, no houses, not much water, lots of stones. 40 days. That's two times what we counted. A long time.

Jesus went into the desert to think about the kind of person he wanted to be, and a bad man called the devil asked him difficult questions, and God helped Jesus to answer them. And after 40 days Jesus came out of the desert, ready to find some friends and work for God.

Ruth Burgess, Spill the Beans

You're my refuge (Psalm 91)

You who live in the Most High's presence,
who camp in Almighty God's shadow, say this:
God, you're my refuge.
I trust you and I'm safe.

God will rescue you from hunters' traps,
heal you from deadly diseases.
God will protect you with outstretched arms.
Under God's wings you will be safe.
God's faithfulness is your armour.
God, you're my refuge.
I trust you and I'm safe.

We live in a dangerous world, great God,
too big for us to protect ourselves.
We offer ourselves to you, open ourselves to you,
and you keep us safe.
So we pray for the whole world,
for all people facing dangers …
and we pray for those who lay down their lives …
and we pray for our leaders …
May we all find rest in your truth, your freedom.

Silence

Don't fear anything – not the monsters in the night,
not the arrows flying in the daytime,
not disease stalking you in the darkness,
not disaster erupting at high noon.
Even if a thousand are struck down in front of you,
or ten thousand drop like flies beside you,
none of it will overwhelm you.
You will watch the destruction of the wicked,
but you won't be destroyed.
Because God is your refuge,
because you are at home with the Most High,
evil cannot have you, destruction can't get through your door.
God, you're my refuge.
I trust you and I'm safe.

We know we aren't supposed to fear, Most High,
but the world is a frightening place.
We offer ourselves to you, open ourselves to you,
and you lift us past danger.
So we pray for those facing the monsters of this life,
losing hope, all alone …
and we pray for those struggling
with illness, infirmity and mortality …
and we pray for those facing death, destruction and grief …
May we bring your safety, shelter
and comfort to carry them past all this.

Silence

God has given Divine messengers orders
to guard you wherever you go.
They will catch you when you stumble, and never let you fall.
You will walk all over lions and deadly snakes
and kick young lions and serpents out of your way.
God promises:
'I will protect those who get to know me
and learn to trust me.
I will come running when they call.
I'll stand by them through all the trouble.
I'll get them out of trouble and give them glory.
I'll be with them through a good long life,
giving them a heaping portion of salvation.'
God, you're my refuge.
I trust you and I'm safe.

We know we should go out boldly in your name, Saving God,
but, while we trust you, we don't trust ourselves.
We offer ourselves to you, open ourselves to you,
and you make us Christ's body.
So we pray for your holy Church …
May we live in the boldness you plant in our hearts.

Silence

God, you're my refuge.
I trust you and I'm safe.

James Hart Brumm

Foxes and hens (Luke 13:31–35)

Do you know any stories about foxes?

Fantastic Mr Fox?
Fox in Socks?
The Tale of Mr Tod?
Rosie's Walk?

There are lots of them.

And in most of them the fox is a real crafty character.

Do you know that Jesus called someone a fox?

Can you guess who it was?

It was King Herod – not the King Herod who tried to kill Jesus when he was a baby – but another King Herod, his son.

So, this is a story about a fox.

Do you know any stories about chickens?

Henny Penny?
The Fox-Busters?
Chicken Licken?

There are lots of them as well.

Did you know that Jesus once said he'd like to be like a chicken?

Well, he did.

So this is a story about a fox and a chicken.

Here it comes.

One day, Jesus was on his way to Jerusalem when some teachers came to him with a warning.

'You'd better get away from here,' they said.

'You know King Herod?
You won't remember, but his dad, King Herod the Great, wanted to kill you.
Well, this King Herod is his son, he's called Herod Antipas, and he wants to kill you as well.'

Jesus wasn't scared.
He looked at the teachers.
'You go and give that fox King Herod a message from me,' he said.
'Tell him I'm busy.
I've got lots of work to do.
And I won't stop until I've finished.
And you tell him I'm coming to Jerusalem where he lives.
I'm not running away.'

The teachers were a bit shocked.
Calling the king a fox didn't seem to them a very good idea.
And they were probably too scared to tell King Herod
what Jesus had said about him.
Or maybe they did.

Jesus loved the people of Jerusalem.
Sometimes they got things wrong.
Sometimes they listened to the wrong people.
Sometimes they ran around not knowing what to do.
But Jesus loved them.

'What are you like, Jerusalem?' said Jesus.
'I'd like to be a big warm feathery mother hen,
so that I could gather your children under my wings
and keep them safe and strong.
But you wouldn't let me do it, Jerusalem.
And I can't help you if you won't let me.'

And when Jesus thought about the people of Jerusalem
he was sad because he knew that they wouldn't listen to him
or let him help them.

So that's today's story, quite a short one:
a story about a dangerous fox and a big warm feathery mother hen.

And not many people know this story.

But you do now, don't you?

Ruth Burgess, Spill the Beans

Lament for Jerusalem (and other cities)

Tune: 'Skippin' barfit through the heather' (Scots traditional)

Jesus on the hillside stood
wracked with tears and bitter grieving,
crying out to souls he loved
as a mother loves her children.

'Dearly blessed, Jerusalem,
how I longed to bring you healing
and give you shelter in my arms
as a mother shields her children.

All the words I offered you,
all the gifts I would have given;
all your choices closed but one –
ruined walls and desolation.'

Other cities, other years,
endless ruined generations
moving God to helpless tears
as a mother mourns her children.

Roddy Cowie

See: https://audioboom.com/posts/6057920-lament-for-jerusalem-and-other-cities

Light and deliverance (Psalm 27)

God is light and deliverance for me:
Who is there to fear?

God is safety for me:
Who is there to dread?

When forces of evil come after me to devour me,
it is my enemies, the bullies, who fall to pieces.
If an army lays siege to me, my heart will be calm.
If war is waged against me, I will be confident.

You are our light in a dark world, O God,
keeping us safe and freeing us from fear.
And so we praise you and thank you for all the light you bring us,
all the blessings of this life …

Silence

I'm asking God for one thing, looking for only one thing:
To live in God's house all my days;
to contemplate God's beauty
and study at God's feet.

In the tough times God shelters me,
gives me space in God's tent,
sets me high on a rock.
With my head lifted higher than my enemies around me,
I offer gifts in that tent,
shouting with joy,
singing loud and long for God!

You are our light in a dark world, O God,
and you gather, protect and preserve us
to shine that light through us.
So we pray for your Holy Church …
Let your light shine brightly in us.

Silence

Hear me when I cry for help, God.
Be good to me and answer!

My heart tells me to seek God, so I am seeking;
don't hide from me.
Don't turn away from me.
Don't toss me out or abandon me,
not when you have been so good to me, my deliverer!
Why, even if my mum and dad abandon me,
God will hold on to me.

Teach me your way and show me the safe path, O God.
Don't give me up to my enemies,
the liars, the ones threatening violence.

You are our light in a dark world, O God,
but the darkness still confronts us.
Watch over those who are in places of conflict and danger …
Watch over the homeless, the helpless, the imprisoned …
Watch over those far from home and families,
and those who are alone …
Watch over those struggling with illness, infirmity and mortality …
Watch over those who lead us: may they lead us in your way.
Be our light, our deliverance, our safety, now and always.

Silence

I am sure that I will discover God goodness
springing up from living ground.
Wait for God;
be strong, take heart and wait for God.

You are our light in a dark world, O God,
and we trust in your light,
and so we wait for you.

James Hart Brumm

Second chance (Luke 13:1–9)

Jesus talked to his disciples about sin.

Some people thought that there were little sins, big sins and bigger sins.

Some people thought that the bigger your sin the more you got punished.

Some people boasted about being the biggest sinner.

Some people thought that children could be punished for things their parents had done wrong.

Jesus talked to his disciples about sin.

And he told them that sin is sin, wrong is wrong. Whatever you've done, you need to say sorry and be forgiven.

And then he told them a story:

A man had a fig tree planted in his vineyard.

When the man came to look for fruit on the tree there was none.

The man called his gardener.

'See here!' he said. 'For three years I have come looking for fruit on this fig tree, and still I find none. Cut it down! It's a waste of good soil.'

The gardener replied, 'Sir, let it alone for one more year until I dig around it and put manure on it. If it bears fruit next year, well and good; but if not, you can cut it down.'

Strange story ......

Lots of questions ......

What's this story got to do with sin and forgiveness?

Is this story an episode of Jerusalem Radio, *Gardeners' Question Time*?

Maybe it's a story about second chances?

What do you think?

Ruth Burgess, Spill the Beans

The master is coming tomorrow (Luke 13:1–9)

It was a quiet day and down in the vineyard the grapevines were whispering to each other:

The master is coming tomorrow
The master is coming tomorrow
The master is coming tomorrow sssssshhhhhh

The master is coming tomorrow to look at the grapes on our branches
The master is coming tomorrow to look at the grapes on our branches
The master is coming tomorrow to look at the grapes on our branches ssshhhhh

We need to be ready for the master
We need to be ready for the master
We need to be ready for the master sssssshhhhhhh

In the corner of the vineyard was a small fig tree. Nobody knew why a fig tree had been planted in the vineyard, but it had. The fig tree heard the grapevines whispering to each other and she was very sad. The grapevines were full of big purple grapes but there were no figs on the fig tree's branches. The little fig tree knew why. The grape vines grew quickly and in a few years were full of fruit. Fig trees grow more slowly. The little fig tree wasn't old enough yet to grow figs.

Next morning the grapevines were whispering again:

The master is coming today
The master is coming today
The master is coming today sssssshhhhhh.

The master is coming today to look at the grapes on our branches
The master is coming today to look at the grapes on our branches
The master is coming today to look at the grapes on our branches ssshhhhh

We are ready for the master
We are ready for the master
We are ready for the master sssssshhhhhh

At dinnertime the master came into the garden. His gardener was with him. They walked up and down in between the vines looking at the big juicy grapes. The master was pleased. When they came to the corner of the vineyard they went over to look at the little fig tree.

The master walked round the little fig tree and he was cross. He said to the gardener. 'See here! For three years I have been coming to look at this fig tree. It still has no fruit on it! It's no good! Cut it down!'

The gardener, who knew all about little fig trees, thought for a moment and then he said to the master, 'Sir, let it alone for one more year, until I dig round it, and put manure on it to help it grow. If it hasn't got any fruit on it next year, then you can cut it down.'

The master nodded and walked towards the vineyard gate. The gardener smiled and he whispered into the fig tree's leaves, 'Don't worry, little fig tree, next year you will be ready to grow fruit and the master will find figs on your branches.'

That evening the grapevines were whispering again:

The master came today
The master came today
The master came today sssshhhhhh

The master came today to look at the grapes on our branches
The master came today to look at the grapes on our branches
The master came today to look at the grapes on our branches sssshhh

We were ready for the master
We were ready for the master
We were ready for the master ssshhhh

And the little fig tree smiled to herself and then she rustled all her leaves and shouted:

NEXT YEAR
NEXT YEAR
NEXT YEAR
I WILL HAVE FIGS ON MY BRANCHES
I WILL BE READY FOR THE MASTER. HOORAY!

Ruth Burgess, Spill the Beans

Note: The sssshhhhhh could be whoooosh, depending on what sound you think grapevines make!

I search for you (Psalm 63)

God! You're my God!
I search for you!
My soul thirsts for you!
My body craves you
as it craves refreshment in the desert.

That's why I'm in your sanctuary,
gazing at your power and glory.
That's why I sing your praises –
because your loving-kindness is better than life.
That's why I spend my whole life blessing you,
lifting up my hands and shouting your praises.
Our souls are filled; you have given us a feast.
Now our mouths sing joyful praises.
You have gathered us and fed us, great God,
nourishing us for your new life.
You have gathered us and fed us,
and now we sing your praises,
and we offer you our prayers. *(Psalm 63:1–5)*

God! You're my God!
I search for you!

My soul thirsts for you!
My body craves you
as it craves refreshment in the desert.

I lie in bed at night, pondering your grace in the wee hours;
you are always there for me,
and I can sing joyfully, safe under your wings.
My soul holds you tightly,
and your strong hand holds me up. *(Psalm 63:1,6–8)*

You are always there for us, and we are safe,
and so we pray for our world …
for those who lay down their lives …
for those who lead us …

Silence

And so we pray for those who especially need care …

Silence

And so we pray for ourselves and all your Church …

Silence

God! You're my God!
I search for you!
My soul thirsts for you!
My body craves you
as it craves refreshment in the desert.

Our leaders should choose God;
faithful followers will be singing praises
when lying mouths are silenced. *(Psalm 63:1, 9–11)*

You are our God.
You keep us safe and bring salvation,
and so we pray to you.

James Hart Brumm

Lost and found (Luke 15:11–32)

This was written in Notting Hill in the 1980s. Update as you see fit.

Narrator: There was once a woman who had two daughters. One day one of them said:

First daughter: Mum, I really need some money. You said you were saving up till each of us got married. Can I have my share now?

Narrator: They lived in a village. She'd heard about the bright lights in the city and she wanted to break out, be different, have a good time. So the mother went down to the building society, drew out the money and gave it to her daughter, who bought a one-way ticket to the big city.

There was plenty to spend money on: clothes, pubs, clubs – not to mention food and somewhere to stay. But things were more expensive in the city. Before she knew it, her money had run out. She couldn't pay the rent. She could barely afford a cup of tea. She had to sleep rough. She tried to get a job, but her shabby appearance and lack of any proper address didn't help. She was hungry all the time. Once she got a job washing up in a seedy hotel, and was tempted to eat the greasy scraps that were thrown in the bin.

Some of the others who were on the streets turned to prostitution. She sat in the underpass with a bit of cardboard on which she'd scrawled HOMELESS AND HUNGRY and a few people threw her coins. Then she came to her senses.

First daughter: Here I am asking people for charity, when my mum is always giving money to famine relief. She has a job too. She sometimes even pays for a service wash at the laundrette. She might pay me to clean the house … I'm going home. I'll say to my mother, 'Mum, what I did was wrong, don't call me your daughter any more. But give me a job.'

Narrator: So she set off, hitching and walking, all the way home. She was still at the end of the street, when her mother looked out and saw her lost child! Her heart went out to her daughter, and she ran to meet her, hugged and kissed her. The daughter said:

First daughter: Mum, what I did was wrong. Don't act as if nothing happened. I'm not your little girl any more.

Narrator: But the mother led her indoors, ran a bath, got clean underwear and her best dress out of the wardrobe, and put these ready for her child to wear. She said to one of the neighbours:

Mother: Take this money and get me an oven-ready turkey.

First daughter: I'm a vegetarian.

Mother: Well, a deluxe pizza then, and a bottle of wine – look, my daughter might as well have been dead, and she's come back to life. She's come home. She was lost and we've found her again.

Narrator: Now the older daughter, who was living at home and going to college and working hard, getting good grades, she was on her way home. She heard the stereo from the end of the street, and saw people running in and out of the house. She thought:

Second daughter: Mum's flipped her lid.

Narrator: She grabbed an excited neighbour.

Second daughter: What happened?

Neighbour: Your sister has come home and your mum's throwing a party because she's back safe and sound.

Narrator: The older sister was furious. She leaned against the wall and refused to go into the house. Their mother came out and begged her, but she retorted:

Second daughter: Didn't you notice me all these years? Don't I matter? I'm the reliable one. I got a Saturday job and gave you something every week. I never disobeyed you. And you never even let me invite my friends round for a party. Now look what happens when *she* comes home! She's spent all your savings. She's been living it up. She's been doing goodness-knows-what in the city. She's probably caught something really nasty ... and you throw a party.

Mother: My love ...

Narrator: Said the mother.

Mother: You are very close to me. I share everything with you. Won't you share this celebration with me? Your sister was dead and she's come back to life. She was lost and now she's found.

Jan Sutch Pickard

Who would have thought?

Who would have thought that you were a party God:
a God who loved a celebration;
a God who loved the sound of laughter –
and would belt out a song from the karaoke machine;
a God who could strut his stuff on the dance floor
and do an eightsome reel with the rest of us?

Who would have thought that you were a patient God,
who watched, and waited and fretted,
when we had turned our back on you;
who saw us squander our life and treasures
on things we thought were important,
only to realise that, in the end,
they just leave us exhausted, worn out and disillusioned?

Who would have thought that you were a God of love,
who cherished people regardless of their personality,
who gave the clothes off his back to dress us,
the food from his table to feed us,
and the finest jewels from his safe to adorn us,
and who would uncork the best wine from his cellar to welcome us home?

Open our eyes today that we might see you, O God,
not as some far-flung heavenly being,
but as a friend who truly understands us.

Open our ears, that we might hear you in your songs of praise,
or in the whispering voice which tells us that you are near.

Open our mouths that we might speak to you and for you
in our homes and communities,
so that others will know
how wonderful you are.

Liz Crumlish, Spill the Beans

Telling you everything (Psalm 32)

Someone is lucky to have offences forgiven and sins wiped clean.
Someone is truly happy when God finds no guilt, when one's spirit is clear.
When I bottled it all up, my bones wore away under my groans;
your hand was crushing me, day and night;
my life evaporated in the summer sun.
Then I told you everything and hid nothing. *(Psalm 32:1–5a)*

We come to you, telling you everything,
knowing, deep down, that you already know.
We come to you and you wipe everything away,
lifting our burdens.
That is why we can pray to you.
That is why we can thank you for the blessings of life.
We come to you, praying, and hope you hear, God.

Silence

'I will confess my sins to God,' I said,
and right away you forgave my sins and lifted my guilt from me.
That's why all faithful people should keep praying,
so that, when troubles come, we won't be swept up in the flood.
You are my safe hideaway,
sheltering me from trouble,
surrounding me with salvation songs. *(Psalm 32:5b–7)*

We come to you, telling you everything,
knowing, deep down, that you already know.
We come to you and you give us a safe hideaway.
So we pray for our world and all the people in it …
for those who lay down their lives …
for those who lead …

Silence

We pray for those in special need of care, care of all kinds,
and we pray especially for …

Silence

We pray for ourselves, doing our best to be your holy Church …

Silence

We come to you, praying, and we hope you hear, O God.

Silence

I will teach you the way to go,
watching closely and explaining carefully.
Don't be a senseless mule or horse
who has to be harnessed and led.
Evil people suffer all sorts of pain and trouble.
But loving-kindness surrounds us when we trust in God.
Everyone who is innocent should praise God.
And those with pure hearts should sing out! *(Psalm 32:8–11)*

We come to you, telling you everything,
knowing, deep down, you already know.
We come to you, and you restore us,
teach us,
fill us with song.
We come to you, praying, sure that you hear every prayer.

James Hart Brumm

Lazarus and Martha reflect (John 12:1–8)

A dialogue between Lazarus and Martha, following the incident of Mary anointing Jesus. Lazarus should be fairly aggressive throughout. Martha should speak slowly and deliberately, as though trying to be patient and instil calm.

Lazarus: You're not going to tell me you weren't completely embarrassed?!

Martha: You think she took it a bit far?

Lazarus: A bit far? That's an understatement! The house is going to reek of this stuff for days! And letting her hair down like that – a respectable woman! Does she want a reputation?

Martha: Her heart was in the right place.

Lazarus: Her heart? What about her head? What about putting her brain in gear for once?

Martha: You know how she is.

Lazarus: I know how she is all right. Emotional. Impulsive. Embarrassing.

Martha: She didn't embarrass Jesus.

Lazarus: He's already got all the reputation he needs.

Martha *(with an edge of irritation):* Yes, I hear he's got quite some reputation for raising the dead. He got so emotional at your grave, it made him impulsive enough to call you back to us, instead of facing the grief like a man. How embarrassing!

Lazarus: *(stunned silence, grasping for a good comeback)* Jesus is hardly one to avoid facing what grieves him.

Martha: Neither is Mary.

Lazarus: What?

Martha: The smell did it. The smell of this perfume. It took me right back to your grave. Standing there hearing Jesus crying for us to open it. All I could think was the smell will be so bad by now – the smell of death. I didn't need to see you to know. The first waft of the tomb air told me. Not stale and stomach-churning, but impossibly fresh and clear. Now, this perfume … a smell so intense, we're all spooked … this is the smell of death, not past but about to come … they're after him, and we're all pretending it's not happening. Who's the only one with the guts to face it, to be real with him? … Mary.

Lazarus: Oh please! You women! The one with the guts and the reality check is Judas! He's right – we could have raised a year's wages selling that nard! Poor Enan and Dinah right here in Bethany could have got back on their feet and stopped their begging! Nathan could have bought his vineyard back! Ithamar could have provided for his sister's orphans. But no, all those chances go squandered, utterly squandered – and this house stinks of nothing but waste.

Martha: She adores Jesus. I wish I could love so wastefully. I wish we all could. What a world this would be.

The dialogue could be followed by a time of conversation where people are invited to share with a neighbour, 'How do you feel about the perspectives portrayed by Lazarus and Martha? Who gets your sympathy and why?'

Jo Love, Spill the Beans

Around a table

We thank you, God,
for meals shared around a table,
for birthday cake and Christmas turkey,
fish and chips out of the paper,
Indian and Chinese carry-outs,
pizza and pasta,
kebabs and chicken nuggets –
or our favourite home-cooked meal.

We thank you, God,
for the friends who join us at the table.
For the laughter,
for stories and adventures shared,
for lessons learned,
for the shared highlights of our day.

We thank you, God,
for the love that grew around a table:
a candle-lit dinner for two,
a celebration with friends,
a reunion with family members from far away.

We thank you, God,
for the fellowship around a table,
for forgiveness offered and received,
bread and wine shared in faith,
for hope rekindled like a burning flame within us.

For all that you give us,
we thank you, God.
Amen

Spill the Beans

Filled with laughter (Psalm 126)

When God made everything better for Zion,
it was as if we had all been dreaming.
Our mouths were filled with laughter;
our tongues were filled with joyful shouts.
All the peoples around us said,
'God has made greatness for them.'
God has made greatness for us, and we are joyful. *(Psalm 126:1–3)*

God, you have made greatness for us;
greatness in our lives, greatness in our hearts.
We praise you and thank you for your presence with us,
for your gift of greatness,
for all the ways you make everything better for us, each and every day.

And we pray for you to fill us again.
God, make everything better again;
restore us like streams in the southern desert.
Let those who planted with tears
harvest while singing praises.
Let those who cry while carrying their seed
bring in the crops while loudly praising. *(Psalm 126:4–6)*

God, we need you to make everything better.
We need you to come and restore us.
We pray for the world and all the people in …
and for those women and men who lay down their lives …
and for those who lead us …
We need you to come.
We pray for you to fill us again.

Silence

God, we need you to make everything better.
We need you to come and restore us.
We pray for those in special need of nurture today …
We need you to come.
We pray for you to fill us again.

Silence

God, we need you to make everything better.
We need you to come and restore us.
We pray for your Son's body, your holy Church …
We need you to come.
We pray for you to fill us again.

Silence

God, we need you to make everything better.
We need you to come and restore us.
We know you hear all our prayers,
and so, hear us now.

James Hart Brumm

General resources for Lent

Rethinking Lent

Fasting

It is time for us to review our celebration of Lent.

It is associated with fasting, self-deprivation, self-punishment. Jesus' disciples did not observe official religious fasting days. He was taken to task. His response is reported in Matthew, Mark and Luke: *'The wedding guests cannot mourn as long as the bridegroom is with them, can they? The days will come when the bridegroom will be taken away from them – that will be the time to fast.'*

If Jesus' words are taken seriously, it is Easter Saturday which is an appropriate day for fasting, not the whole lead-up to Easter.

The period of fasting leading up to Easter is at present associated with Jesus' fasting in the wilderness in preparation for his mission. But the whole of his earthly life led up to and was fulfilled in his death and resurrection.

We cannot go through what Jesus went through. What we can do is take the signals for true living which he gave in his earthly life and be instructed by them for our own growth in faith.

The bridegroom is now with us as a living presence as we move through Lent! It is in the presence of the bridegroom that we prepare to understand more deeply, and assimilate into our own lives the character of his earthly life and the empowering he is willing to provide for our growth in the kind of faith he displayed.

When, coming down from the Mount of Transfiguration, Jesus found the disciples unable to cure the epileptic boy, he did so, saying in the account of the 'Authorised' version of the Bible that it would take 'prayer and fasting' to effect a cure. Modern translations omit 'and fasting', or include it as a footnote. It was probably added by a copyist.

Fasting is associated with self-abnegation, doing without, in order to feel on our pulses the suffering of people who are so often deprived of the abundant life Jesus Christ willed for them – robbed by cruel circumstance or by human sin in which we all share. Isaiah warns about fasting being a form of self-abasement which has no practical outcome. If fasting has no practical consequences in producing a just society it is a form of self-delusion:

'Why do we fast, but you do not see?
Why humble ourselves, but you do not notice?'

'Look, you serve your own interests on your fast day
and oppress all your workers …
Is not this the fast that I choose:
to loose the bonds of injustice,
to undo the thongs of the yoke,
to let the oppressed go free,
and break every yoke?
Is it not to share your bread with the hungry,
and bring the homeless poor into your house;
when you see the naked to cover them,
and not to hide yourself from your own kin?

Then your light shall break forth like the dawn,
and your healing shall spring up quickly …' (Is 58)

We are not to tighten our belts to feel others' suffering on our pulses, but to do with less so that the hungry may eat.

Doing justice to Lent

Jesus Christ's earthly being and work affords resources to all who look for growth in faith. Lent covers forty weekdays from Ash Wednesday to Holy Saturday. In nature that is a time of preparation and promise leading to fruitfulness. That is the note to strike in our celebration.

Lent comes from the Old English *'lengten'*. It indicates the *lengthening out* of daylight in the springtime, the burgeoning of life, a time when light overcomes the darkness of winter, an opening out to the work and growth of seedtime.

It can thus be related to the world's springtime, when the Light of the world took on 'the power of darkness', moving to the crucifixion, and bested it, leaving an empty tomb. From that point the 'lengthening out' took place in

Jerusalem, then in Judea and Samaria, then to the ends of the earth. We can all make growth in such a springtime.

For there is work to be done in making our own what Jesus Christ accomplished for us (Eph 4).

But how? Lent and Strictly

Mary Magdelene's instinctive word for Jesus at the tomb was 'Rabboni', 'Teacher'. In the dance of life, he is Lord of the dance, *the present Lord*. Through the Holy Spirit, his earthly life is brought alive, made available. His way is made known to all who are willing to take to the floor with him. He is willing to take on the veriest tyros. Lent is a time for it. What are we waiting for? We can get hints from *Strictly Come Dancing*, where those proficient in the art take on tyros and bring out the best in them.

Personally, and in small groups which may meet, say, once a week, we can learn the steps of faith from the Master and become more proficient in living.

There are different dances, partners, occasions, as is indicated by the Sydney Carter hymn 'Lord of the dance'. Enter into Jesus' flair for movement, which is both gracious (graceful) and expressive of life's demand and promise. Think of moving with him through his acts of daring, of healing and blessing, of self-giving sacrifice, learning, learning, learning from the Master of Life.

Ian M Fraser

Clare's grandad (A children's story about death)

Clare's grandad was looking forward to his birthday. He was going to be ninety years old. There was going to be a cake with ninety candles. It was going to be a big cake. Clare enjoyed spending time with her grandad – he loved his garden and his greenhouse and sometimes he told her stories about when he was a little boy.

Clare's grandma was nearly as old as their grandad. She was 89. Next year she would have a cake with ninety candles too.

One day Clare's mum had a phone call. Grandad was in hospital. Clare's mum left Clare with her dad and went to the hospital to see grandad. When Clare's mum came home she looked sad. She told Clare that the doctors had said that grandad was very poorly. He had something called pneumonia.

Two days later her mum took Clare to the hospital to see grandad. Clare's grandma was there too. Grandad looked tired but he smiled at Clare and gave her a kiss.

That night grandad died. Grandma and one of the nurses were with him.

The next day all the family met to talk about grandad. The minister came around too. There was going to be a service in the church to say goodbye to grandad. It was called a funeral. Everyone told the minister stories about grandad. Clare talked about the stories grandad used to tell her, and she told the minister that grandad had taught her how to play draughts, but she had never beaten him.

Two of Clare's friends came around to the house to be with her – she was glad. She told them about the funeral and she asked her mum if they could come too, as they had loved grandad as well.

Lots of people came to the church for the funeral. There were grandad's friends, and people who had worked with him, and people from the bowling club, and grandad's and grandma's neighbours. And all grandad's family were there. And Clare's friends were there with their mums and dads.

At the funeral grandad's friends and family carried his body in a box, called a coffin, into the church. The minister told them that the funeral was a chance to talk about grandad's life, to listen to some words from the Bible and to talk to God about grandad, and about how they were feeling. Some people laughed when the minister told one of grandad's stories. Some people looked sad and cried. They sang one of grandad's favourite songs. The minister had asked Clare what her grandad was like, and Clare had said that grandad was kind, that he told great stories and that he loved growing potatoes and sunflowers. When the minister was talking about grandad she told people what Clare had said, and people smiled.

After the funeral, Clare and her family took grandad's body to the crematorium. Clare's mum had told her about this. Grandad's body was old and not working properly and now that grandad had died he no longer needed his body. They would leave grandad's body at the crematorium and it would be burnt. Then a little later they would collect the ashes from grandad's body, and as a family they could decide where to put them: maybe in a place where grandad liked to walk, maybe in his garden.

When grandad's family had come back from the crematorium they joined all the other people who had been at the funeral in a local hotel for cakes and tea. Clare went and found her friends and they talked about the funeral and Clare told them about the crematorium.

Clare was glad that her friends had been with her at the funeral. It was good to have them there, as well as her family. She knew that they would be able to talk with her about grandad when she wanted to remember him. It's good to have friends.

Ruth Burgess, Spill the Beans

Useful resources:

It is healthy and normal to speak with children and young people about death and what happens when someone dies. It should not be a mystery.

These resources can help:

'That's what a friend is', from *Sing To Make You Feel Good*, by Fischy Music

Michael Rosen's Sad Book, Michael Rosen and Quentin Blake, Walker Books

Grandad's Ashes, Walter Smith, Jessica Kingsley Publishers

A season for more

It is the custom to treat Lent as the season of less.

But over the years, I have come to see this time as a season for more. So here is what I am hoping to do during this holy time:

Spend more time in *silence*. And this means silence from virtual noise as well.

Spend more time *reading* than watching television. Oh, there are those good shows that I'll still catch, but so much of the time the machine is just on – talk about junk food!

Spend more time *outside* – so that I am not always chained to my desk (or computer); so I don't drop into my easy chair the minute I get home. Yes, being with Dusty my dog gets me outside, and this often turns into sacred time, but I could also go outside to read. I could go out on the deck and be mesmerised by the night sky on crisp nights. I could sit on the front step and simply watch and be. I could take that five minute walk that puts me in the park near the church, or in the woods near the house, and quietly savour God's creation.

There is so much *more* I could do during this season of discipleship to become a more faithful follower of Jesus. I hope I do.

Thom M Shuman

A long forty days of silence

A couple of years ago
I decided to observe Lent by turning off the car radio.
It wasn't easy.
It was a long forty days of silence.
I missed the entertainment, the music, the distraction, the weather
and even hearing the traffic reports.
There were days I would get in the car after work
and desperately want to listen to the radio for the long drive home.

Yet, I persisted.
I found this became a time to sit in silence,
or to sing,
or sometimes even pray aloud.

The car became a different space,
and it seemed as if time passed in a different way.
Without hearing news stories of events that took place recently,
I was stuck in the present,
forced to pay more attention to my own mind,
the cars around me
and the road I was travelling.
I was alone,
desperately trying to remember
that we are never truly alone.

Fiona van Wissen

It's easy to say sorry

It's easy to say sorry
when we don't think it's our fault
but want words to turn down the heat.

It's easy to offer regret
for unintended consequences
we are convinced couldn't be foreseen.

It's easy to apologise
if all involved do the same –
nothing to lose, and we might gain.

Who minds acting contrite today
when tomorrow is another day
where we will keep on doing the same?

Let us therefore not pray
I'm sorry.
I apologise.
I regret.

Let us pray instead:

Reveal to us, God,
the extent of what we have done.

Provoke us, God,
until we understand the hurt.

Inspire us, God,
to see how it's possible
to live by your principles.

Transform us, God,
holding us tight until we believe
in fresh starts
and the value of trying again.
Amen

Katherine Fox

Dear God

Dear God,
more than father,
more than mother.
God fully ours, and just as much for neighbours, and foreigners,
and whether we like it or not.

It's good to be here.
To gather in a gathering that strives after the truth
that all who come in peace
are indeed welcome.

To be part of a party
where beauty and wonder have space and time.

To have set aside time.
Earmarked the hour.
And for what?

What's in it for us?
What's our pay?
What's our reward?

God who, it seems, in Christ, loves questions …
What do we gain
to hear your teaching,
to care for your people,
to put behind us the wrong we have chosen,
to know forgiveness?
What good does it do us
to do good and serve others?
What help is it to make a new start?
And then once more?

What benefit could possibly accrue
from placing our life in your hands,
and our hand in your hand?
What profit from a partnership
of heaven and earth?

Dear God. We can't see it.
Though sometimes we catch a glimpse.
And find forgiveness, and trip over the kindness
of those around us.
We can't see it.
But Jesus teaches us to pray ...

Our Father ...

David J.M. Coleman

This is the season

This is the season of
waiting,
of tipping on the edge of life:
a seed planted in furrowed soil,
but will it grow?
Staring at earth, pondering its riches,
nostrils earth-scented in morning dew.
Waiting ...

This is the season of
risk,
watching as the seed turns, shivers, cracks.
Praying the precious root will find purchase,
and not be found.

This is the season of
patience,
nourishment and care.
What will follow will be
bright colours, flowers and taste,
the giddy harvest.
For now, in quiet, we find peace.

Now is a season of prayer,
of waiting and relying,
of knowing the future is in the Creator's hands.
Forces beyond our
control
nurture the seed, if we let them.
This is when we depend,
and are taught to depend.

A green tip will push through the earth,
and we can say:
we waited,
we took the risk,
we were patient,
we prayed,
we depended.

Kira Taylor

Annunciation

Mary

Mary lived a long time ago. One day Mary met an angel. The angel had a message for Mary.

'Mary,' said the angel, 'you are a wonderful person. God loves you.'

Mary had never seen an angel before and she was frightened.

'Don't be frightened, Mary. I have nothing but Good News for you!' said the angel, who was called Gabriel.

Mary still didn't say anything.

'I have a message: God loves you and God wants you to be the mother of Jesus, God's son.'

Mary couldn't think of anything to say because she didn't understand what the angel meant.

'Mary, trust God,' said the angel. 'God will take care of you.'

Mary still remained silent.

'Jesus is going to be a great person. He will show everyone what God is like. Will you be Jesus' mother?'

Mary still didn't understand, but she knew she trusted God, and quietly and softly, just like a whisper, she said one word: 'Yes.'

Spill the Beans

I wanted to say no

I wanted to say no to God. I was not ready to become a mum. I was too young, and Joseph had only just proposed to me. It was all too soon, and I wanted to say no.

No to having a baby, no to motherhood, no to losing my shape, no to the gossip that would surely begin the moment the bump began to show. No to the people who would talk about me, turn away from me and call me names behind my back, or shout abuse in my face. No to all these things and more!

I wanted to say no because ... well, because I was just a wee lassie with no money, no status, no nothing, and surely God would want someone more important than me to bear his child. Joseph and I didn't even have a home of our own yet. We had no money even to buy the essentials – and so what kind of life could we have provided for God's son?

I wanted to say no because I was not sure how Joseph would react to the news I was pregnant. We had hardly kissed up until then. He might have disowned me and turned his back on me and the baby. In fact I could just imagine me trying to tell Joseph I am pregnant. 'Hey, Joseph, I'm pregnant and going to have a baby. Now don't worry, this will be God's son!' I mean what young man would have believed me – even I wouldn't have believed me with that story!

I wanted to say no, because I was afraid of the future, afraid of the pain of motherhood, afraid that people wouldn't understand.

But how do you say no to the Holy God, the God Almighty and the Everlasting Father? How do you say no to the God who has brought down kings and emperors and mighty armies?

How could I say no to a God who knows my heart and my mind and circumstances? How could I say no to a God who loves me and cares for me and has promised to watch over me? How could I say no to a God who has surely blessed me, and honoured me in this way?

I wanted to say no, but I couldn't, and my yes became the promise of the future we all share in.

Thanks be to God that he has chosen me, and you, to say yes.

Spill the Beans

The morning began quietly

The morning began quietly enough.
Nothing in the early sun gave away
the impact of the unique act of love
that held our world's redemption in its sway.

Among the ordinary and routine
essential tasks she daily undertook,
Mary allowed her Lord to intervene.
No one noticed how all creation shook.

And later did she think it all a dream:
the angel and the penetrating joy?
In Nazareth, waiting, did it sometimes seem
she carried not the Word but just a boy.

Doubt's shadows scattered on that hallowed night
when she first cuddled him, our Lord of Light.

Mary Hanrahan

Waiting

Mary's dream

God, I am waiting,
waiting for your coming
into my life …

God, I am expecting –
I can't really believe it,
me bringing you to the world.

Give me patience
and courage as I wait,
hope and work for your glory,

for the coming
of your kingdom
through Jesus, your son,

born in me, living with me,
doing great things for you,
through the Holy Spirit,

who brought your peace,
assurance and, above all, joy
to my life, today, for everyone.

Our dream

God, we are waiting,
waiting for your coming
into our lives.

God, we are expecting,
hoping to see you
at work in the world.

Give us patience
to keep on waiting,
hoping and working

for the coming
of your kingdom,
through Jesus our Lord –

born as a baby in Bethlehem,
living, dying and rising,
reigning with you and the Holy Spirit –

bringing us life and love and peace,
this day, and every day,
to the end of time.

Carol Dixon

Mothering Sunday

Christ who loves us

Christ who loves us
as a mother hen her chicks,
grant to all mothers and fathers
such love for their children
that their care is never denied,
their needs always tended
and their development into freedom
encouraged, protected and guided
with wisdom, truth and understanding
in order for them to attain their full potential
with security and confidence
and thus be enabled to grow into maturity
to become the people they were meant to be.

Bless too those who are orphaned,
all who look after them
and the parents who adopt them,
that they may grow up with love,
wisdom and caring nurture
into their full humanity within a loving family.

Terry Garley

Mothering God

(Tune: 'Epiphany hymn')

Mothering God, your protection surrounds us,
taking away all our worry and fear.
Nurturing God, may we always believe you,
trusting your promise you'll always be near.

Mothering God, there are times when the darkness
threatens our faith in the truth of your love.
Come to us, then, with the power of your Spirit,
fierce as a tigress, yet soft as a dove.

Mothering God, bring us out of the darkness
into the light of your mercy and grace,
living each day in full trust and obedience,
holding each other in love's warm embrace.

Janet Pybon

We lift our prayers to you

God of mothers and fathers, young and old, friends and neighbours, be present in the needs of our world.

As we gather on this day of celebration and praise, we are thankful for the many people who mother us and nurture us to grow in faith and wisdom.

Be with the mothers and grandmothers and great-grandmothers among us.

Hold in your tender care all expectant mothers; strengthen and encourage them as they birth new life.

Be especially close to those who would wish to bear children but who cannot; hold them gently on this day, O God, and always.

We pray for foster mothers, adoptive mothers, stepmothers and all those who give love to children from their hearts. For all those who mother others in so many ways, we give you thanks, and ask that you continue to strengthen them with your grace and knowledge.

We pray for all parents and caregivers around the world, especially those who are struggling to find food, shelter and security for their children.

We pray for children and youth throughout the world, remembering particularly those who are in need of mothers and mentors in their lives; and lifting to your tender mercy all those who are struggling with issues of identity: may they know they are loved for who they are and may their world learn to celebrate diversity.

Be with all our young people as they make decisions that will affect their lives; help them to make good choices, we pray.

Today, O God, we celebrate families – all shapes, all sizes, all configurations – and pray that you will bless them with what they need most.

For those who mourn this day, give comfort, we beseech you; we lift for your tender care all those who have recently lost their mums, that you would wrap them in your healing love.

For those who are torn apart by wrongs or by resentment, may the balm of your grace soothe old hurts, salve old fears, unclench old hates, that all may live more fully. May your peace and grace restore them.

Thankful for the love that you bless us with and hopeful in the promise of grace continued, we lift these prayers to you. Amen

Barbara Miller

Sticky fingers, sloppy kisses

Thank you, God, for the privilege of being a *mother/grandmother.*
For the enjoyment of a small child climbing onto my lap for a cuddle.

Thank you for the warmth of their skin, their infectious giggles,
sticky fingers, sloppy kisses;
for their spontaneity and insatiable curiosity about the world around them, their fascination with mini-beasts and how things work.

Thank you for all the love and joy young children bring into our lives. Amen

Kathy Crawford

We pray for God's family

We quieten our minds
we open our hearts
we come as we are
to pray for God's family.

We pray for all our children
wide-eyed and wondering
vulnerable and violated
orphaned and injured
abused and exploited
energetic and enquiring.

Christ of the manger:
receive our prayer

We pray for young people
persevering and passionate
unemployed and aimless
surly and silent
drugged and despairing
laughing and living.

Christ, healer and helper:
receive our prayer

We pray for all parents
believing and hoping
insecure and inadequate
watching and waiting
solitary and sorrowful
listening and loving.

Christ, servant and sufferer:
receive our prayer

We pray for your church
compassionate and caring

daunted and divided
faltering and faithless
staid and stagnant
vibrant and creative
warm and welcoming.

Christ, living and loving:
receive our prayer
Amen

Avis Palmer

Sometimes it's tough being a parent

Sometimes it's tough being a parent!

We pray today for all those who care for children with physical disabilities or learning difficulties.

For mums who struggle daily to provide for their child's special needs and end up completely exhausted and frustrated by night-time.

For parents who struggle to access the help and support they need, or feel humiliated by the stares of strangers when their child 'behaves inappropriately' in public.

We remember parents who are caring for a child who is terminally ill, and are facing great sadness.

We pray for parents who feel helpless as they discover their teenage children are self-harming or taking drugs.

Sometimes it's tough being a parent!

We pray that you will give your strength to all parents who are struggling; and help us, as their church family, to provide support and never judge. Amen

Kathy Crawford

Unsung

Mum was always singing
around the house, as she dusted,
or washed and dried the dishes
and made the dinner;

and when
I did my homework or read, up in my room,
I heard the sound in the distance
and felt a little less alone,
as though I had my very own
Guardian Angel watching over me:
'Wide as the ocean, deep as the deepest sea.'
One day the singing stopped.
I wondered why, then
realised she knew that I had grown up.

I have my own songs now to sing.

Carol Dixon

In my beginning

O God – my God:
Birth-Mother of Creation,
Womb of Life,
Encompassing Love,
in the beginning you were there,
dancing in the darkness,
breaking the waters,
speaking, naming, animating, loving
into light and being and joy.
We worship you!

In my beginning
you were there,

summoning me from the watery depths,
warm hands of welcome outstretched to greet me, cradled to catch me,
naked and vulnerable in the terror of first light.

Gentle Midwife, we cast ourselves on you;
Mother Hen, we shelter under your wing;
Brooding Spirit, we trust in you,
as once again we tiptoe the tightrope path between life and death,
journeying with Jesus to the cross.

Intimate God,
who bears us, who sustains us, who loves us,
you have given us life.
May we live as your body,
loving and caring, reflecting your glory,
offering hope, that all might know
the freedom and joy of your presence. Amen

Louise Gough

Mothering Sunday prayers

Creator God, on this Mothering Sunday
we give thanks for all mothers and for your gift of life.
Let us pause for a moment and hold our mothers,
or those who mothered us,
before you.

What do we remember?
Maybe the sound of her voice,
or the memory of a dress, a meal, a walk,
a special occasion, a smile …

(Pause)

We thank you for the many moments in which our mothers played a part.
Creator God, we thank you for the loving gift of mothers.

Loving, mothering God,
Hear our prayer.

We pray for the people who find today a sad or difficult time.
We pray for families who have lost a partner, a parent or a child.
Loving, mothering God,
Hear our prayer.

We pray for single parents, both mums and dads,
and for grandparents and for extended families.
Loving, mothering God,
Hear our prayer.

We pray for families where children or parents have special needs.
Loving, mothering God,
Hear our prayer.

We pray for families where mental illness has led to a loss of memory and recognition.
Loving, mothering God,
Hear our prayer.

We pray for those who long for a child.
Loving, mothering God,
Hear our prayer.

We thank God for families where children are well
and happy and full of life.
Loving, mothering God,
Hear our prayer.

On this Mothering Sunday,
we give thanks for our Mother Church:
for our experience of being loved by a family
that is as wide and broad as the human race.
Creator God, we thank you for always holding us in the palm of your hand.

We give thanks that we can all practise your mothering gifts
as we live and grow in this family of the church.

Here we can learn to be welcoming and comforting,
to share our experiences,
to listen to each other and to grow in grace and love.

Creator God, on this Mothering Sunday
we give thanks for the gift of mothering
which you have bestowed within us all.
Amen.

Tricia Creamer

We pray also

On this day when we thank God for loving mothers
we pray also for those who do evil:
for parents who deliberately harm their children,
for adults who abuse others – physically, emotionally, sexually,
for those who have tortured and murdered.

We pray for those who judge them and sentence them
and work with them on our behalf.

We pray for those whom they have harmed.

Loving God our maker,
for you there is no them and us:
in you there is justice and hope for all humanity.

Some prayers are hard, God,
this one included.

We offer it in the name of Jesus and in the power of the Holy Spirit.
Amen

Ruth Burgess

Spring in March

Primroses on the Uisken road

Among the dead brambles
on the edge of a ditch
in this bleak wind – right now –
primroses are blooming.

First there was one alone,
a brave promise of new life,
a single star; then ten, a score,
more, more, lifting up their heads:
a constellation, a celebration –
here and now.

Though this wind chills to the bone,
between the thorns and the mud
the rumour of resurrection spreads –
there's no stopping it now.

Jan Sutch Pickard

One more spring

If the good Lord were to come to me this night
and say that I was about to draw my last breath of this earth's air,
I would ask him if I could see yet one more spring;
if one more time I could see the earth green and flower,
watch again the bare outline of trees colour with soft, young green.

I would ask to witness delicate snowdrops
breaking through the last winter snow,
vibrant daffodils heralding the rising of the sun higher in our sky
and the solitary flowering of the blackthorn,
pioneering the return of life to the hedgerow.

I would ask to feel again the sun growing warmer on my face,
to see the retreat of winter's night
and wake again to a brighter, earlier dawn.

I would ask for another morning to hear the blackbird burst into song,
another night to listen for the cry of the tawny owl seeking her mate,
another spring to welcome the swallow's return.

For I will measure my life not by the winters I have endured
but by the springs I have enjoyed;
though I mourn for all that I have watched pass from this life,
I celebrate all the good and beauty that I have seen brought to birth.

For springtime is the renewal of beauty and hope;
it is the power of life overcoming the hold of death;
it is nature's expression of resurrection,
the sign that God brings the renewing of all things.

So, Lord, may I see yet another spring,
that my heart will be filled with joy at its beauty
and my faith renewed through the wonder of the season,
before I enter into that eternal springtime where
You are making all things new.

Simon Taylor

Creator God

Creator God,
we thank you for the beauty of your springtime creation,
awakening buds and blooms,
lengthening blue skies and sunshine.

Awaken hope within us.
Renew us.
May we be refreshed with energy and enthusiasm
to see you in the places where we live
and in the people around us.

Redeemer God,
we thank you for your son, Jesus,
for his parables and teaching,

healing and caring,
for his life and death and resurrection.
Awaken love within us.
Renew us.
May we share your love and care with others.
May we and they come close to you.

Companion God,
we thank you for your Holy Spirit,
for your comfort and guidance,
presence and trust.

Awaken faith within us.
Renew us.
May we share your way and life with others.
May we be a witness to your saving love.

Creator, Redeemer, Companion,
Father, Son and Holy Spirit,
we bring our praise and thanks to you.

Ruth Bowen

I wake and know (St Patrick)

(Tune: 'Slane')

I wake, and know surely my Lord is with me.
I call on the Trinity, one God and three:
The Father who founded the worlds with His word,
The deep flowing Spirit, and Jesus the Lord.

I wake to the grace of my Lord who was born,
Baptised in a river, and beaten and scorned,
And nailed by His hands to the wood of a tree,
And suffered the same death that waits you and me.

I waken and know He is risen in power,
To come in the clouds in the last fearful hour,
When angels will praise Him with fire in their wings,
The reward of His servants, the Judge of all things.

I wake to the beauty and love of great souls
United in prayer with the prophets of old,
Made humble by purity, taught by the wise –
My sisters and brothers who lead me to Christ.

I wake to the sun and the wind in the air,
The speed of the lightning, the splendour of fire,
The depth of the sea and the hardness of stone,
The weight of the earth and the whiteness of snow.

God is my journey and God is my guide.
God is my strength and the shield at my side.
God's wisdom teaches me all I must know.
God's eye is on me wherever I go.

Against my own weakness and evil and fire
Let Christ be my safety and all I desire.
Light high above me, and rock at my feet,
Christ in my own soul and in all souls I meet.

Christ in all places and Christ in all times.
Christ in my body and Christ in my mind.
Christ in all ears and all eyes and all breath.
And Christ the reward that awaits beyond death.

I waken and know that my God is with me.
Secure in His goodness I call on the Three,
Almighty Creator and Spirit and Son.
Be with us for ever, eternally one: Amen

Roddy Cowie

Joseph

(Feast day, 19th March)

It was a shock, and very embarrassing.
Religion had been, for me, a childhood habit:
a reassuring ritual, beautiful music.
I tried to live respectably, doing no harm.
But for this girl it was altogether different.
God had spoken to her, she said, was *in* her, Life itself.

Taken over by God? So where did that leave me?
I shrank from the social censure, mockery, disgrace.
Still, I loved her. Slept on it. Something changed my mind.
I decided to support her, for better or worse,
and the life forming in her without my aid.

Any birth feels like a miracle, I suppose.
Nothing – and then – a person! Maybe, you say,
but plenty of innocents will not survive;
they are born disabled or sick; are deprived, abused or killed.
What can I tell you? I only know what I felt:
When she cradled him in her arms she embraced them all.

Sue Sabbagh

A song for St Cuthbert's Holy Island

(Tune: 'Sussex Carol')

Cuthbert, the humble shepherd saint
and hermit on the Inner Farne,
who lived a simple life of faith,
praised God, and kept his folk from harm.
On Holy Island he worked and prayed
that all might come to God and be saved.

He blessed the cuddy ducks and seals,
and priests and pilgrims called him friend.

The poor and needy sought him out
for help and hope, their lives to mend,
learned to set time apart to pray,
care for others and follow Christ's way.

Still on St Cuthbert's Isle today
we dedicate our lives again:
may strangers come and feel at home,
and all be welcomed in Christ's name.
Praise God for saints who served of old!
May we who serve today be as bold!

Carol Dixon

Note: Based on St Cuthbert's Holy Island Mission Statement:

'We follow the example of St Cuthbert by offering:

a place to be apart with God,
a simple hospitable welcome,
a place of prayer and renewal,
a place where strangers feel at home.'

Wake

I winter-write, by grandchild chased.
'What was it really like?
That static world when every day
changed not from yesterday?'

Facts and things and artefacts
abound on every page.
Winter-depressed, no acts of mine
seem to deserve one line.

Have I existed four score years
and nothing done of note?
Made no response to life's caress?
January answers 'Yes'.

Shocked by the snowdrop carpet,
dazed by the daffodil dance,
something inside me feels the shake
of March on my shoulder, screaming 'Wake'.

There are things I can do in the spring now upon me.
Things I can boast of to the curious child.
The pains of old age may be slow to arrive.
I can do, I can feel, I can love. I'm alive.

Chris Elgood

The new growth of spring

The birds are gathering again
as the ivy on the boundaries
prepares to host their nests,
their eggs and their young.

Light is returning again each day
as dawn arrives slightly earlier
and evening lingers just a little longer,
increasing the time between sunrise and set.

The buds are swelling again
and the first flowers of the year are out –
snowdrops and hellebores, crocuses and heath.
Colour is coming back into the green.

Lent is here again and the lengthening of days.
Easter will come –
still taking its name from earlier times
as the season of the arrival of new life,
with the birth of lambs and chicks,
rabbits and hares and the fresh growth of spring.

But for those who follow in the faith of Christ,
who died that we may live in him,
Easter celebrates his rising from death
and the promise of new life eternally with him.

Terry Garley

A second chance

How often do we get a second chance?
I had one just the other day.
A chance to see the early spring again:
the first leaves,
willow buds opening,
violets everywhere,
some dark trunks, crowns still quite bare,
the faintest green on beach twig tips,
the lightest yellowing canopies of oak.
I enjoyed it as in slow motion once again
in upper Teesdale.

Wake up!
The world is waking up.
Watch.
Listen.
Scent.
Touch.
Quick, you might miss
spring beginning.

Stay awake, alert.
You do not know at what time
the Bridegroom comes!

Liz Gregory-Smith

Palm Sunday

An arrangement

I had known him a lifetime
or so it seemed
and we talked late into the night,
of friends and family,
occupation and freedom,
poetry and politics and God.

When the oil lamps flickered,
we slept.

Usually an early riser,
this morning I woke to the sound
of other people's feet upon the road.
The menacing, steady stamp of soldiers marching,
the unruly rattle of creaking carts,
the heavy plod of a loaded mule;
greetings and cries,
people heading for town,
market day in the city.

Saying goodbye,
a parting request confirmed my fears.
Ruler and Roman, freedom fighter,
Pharisee and friend;
he had to show a different way.
Confrontation and affirmation!
'Of course, of course,' I nodded.
'Take the donkey, any day.'

Avis Palmer

Children's song

(Tune: 'Bunessan')

Jesus is coming!
Joy and excitement,
telling our friends that
he's on his way.
Will you come with us,
leave what you're doing?
Wait at the roadside.
Wonderful day!

Here he comes smiling,
happy to see us.
We wave our branches.
His praises sing.
He told us stories,
valued our friendship.
Join us to welcome
the children's King.

He has passed by now
but we are glowing;
bright joyful faces,
lives not the same.
Sure of his caring,
knowing his kindness,
feeling his blessing,
Christ is his name.

This Sunday morning
echoes of gladness
from Jewish children
reach to our ears.
We add our voices
to the rejoicing.
Jesus is with us,
Love for all years.

Avis Palmer

Palm Sunday collect

O Christ, you entered the city as a poor man,
not in style but simply,
yet still you caused uproar, and questions everywhere;
you drew the expectations of a hungry crowd,
and brought buried conflicts to the light.
May we, who are sometimes swayed by the crowd's approval,
and who often avoid conflict
for fear of its cost to us,
hold fast to the gospel of truth and justice
and follow faithfully in your way of compassion and solidarity
with those who are poor and excluded,
wherever it may lead us.

Kathy Galloway

So many journeys

So many different journeys we've taken in our time together, my son and I.

I remember still that first one, when he was just a tiny spark of life within me, hardly more than an angel's promise, but enough to make his cousin leap in his mother's womb – such a joyous welcome at our journey's end.

And then there was that long, weary journey to Bethlehem when, with every jolting step of the donkey, I wondered how long I could keep him safe in my womb, my precious cargo, enveloped by my body and my love.

And how awful was that frantic journey into Egypt – refugees fleeing from Herod's jealous anger.

I remember, too, our journey back to Nazareth, with his incessant question, 'Are we nearly there yet?' A curious child eager to meet the relatives we'd talked about so much.

Since then we've made so many journeys like this one, to Jerusalem, joining the throngs arriving for the pilgrim feasts. I recall that heart-stopping moment when he was twelve, when on the way back to Galilee we realised he was not with our friends. How I could have slapped him when we found him, relief and anger flooding through me with equal measure!

But none of those journeys could have prepared me for this, and I still can't really grasp what is happening. It should be enough to make any mother's heart swell with pride: to see her son welcomed and feted, greeted like a king, the crowds ecstatic as he passes by, palm branches and cloaks on the road ahead of him.

And yes, I am proud, but also more than a little afraid. I think again of old Simeon's words, 'And a sword shall pierce your soul also.' Truly, with this son of mine, a sword has pierced my soul, yes, more than once. But what did Simeon mean by 'also'? What did his prophecy mean for Jesus?

And what did Jesus mean last night, when he said that Mary had anointed him for burial?

O, Jesus, my beloved son, how I wish I knew what you are thinking as you ride ahead of me into Zion.

Janet Pybon

Here we go

Andy: *(walks on singing, dressed up with his tartan bunnet and scarf)* Here we go, here we go, here we go!

Ada: Naw you'll no, naw you'll no, naw you'll no!

Andy: Aye I will, aye I will, aye I will!

Ada: Just you wait a minute. Where do you think you're going all dressed up? Scotland huv'nae qualified for the European Championships this year.

Andy: But I'm no going to the football. I am going on a parade.

Ada: What kind of parade? Your no going to join in one of those violent demonstrations against the government.

Andy: Naw, Ada, this is a happy parade.

Ada: Is the circus coming to town? Is that why you're all dressed up?

Andy: Naw, it's no the circus that's coming.

Ada: Well, is the Queen coming?

Andy: Naw, the Queen's no coming here either.

Ada: Well, what kind of parade are you going on? The only other parade that happens here is the Orange Walk, and you are no dressed up for that either.

Andy: Well, if you must know, I am going on a church parade to celebrate Easter.

Ada: Well, why are you dressed up like a refugee from the Tartan Army?

Andy: Well, remember the time Jesus marched into Jerusalem riding on a donkey, and the people waved palm branches in the air and sang victory songs?

Ada: Aye, I know that story well. Our church once had a real live donkey and it made a terrible mess on the carpet.

Andy: Well, this year the people in our local churches have decided to have a parade to tell everyone about Jesus, and because we don't have the weather here in *(your location)* for palm branches, the minister said to bring something to wave, so I'm taking my scarf and tammy.

Ada: You mean you're going to parade around the streets of *(your location)* singing songs about Jesus and waving your scarves and banners in the air?

Andy: That's right, Ada, my wee darling – you are certainly catching on to this.

Ada: Can anyone come?

Andy: The more the merrier.

Both: Here we go, here we go, here we go! …

John Murning, Spill the Beans

Script for eleven voices (Luke 19:28–40)

Including at least one child – and two stones!

Narrator: Jesus and his disciples were getting nearer and nearer to Jerusalem. Jesus had tried a few times to tell his disciples what was going to happen to him in Jerusalem but his disciples still didn't understand what he was trying to tell them. They were near Bethany now and Jesus sent two of his disciples ahead with these instructions.

Jesus: Go into the village, and as you enter the village you will see a young donkey tied up by wall. Untie the donkey and bring it back to me. If anybody asks you why you are untying it, tell them Jesus needs it.

First disciple: I don't like this.

Second disciple: What do you mean?

First disciple: I really don't like this.

Second disciple: Don't like what?

First disciple: I don't like going into a strange village to untie a donkey and walk away with it! If that happened in my village, the men who did it wouldn't get out of the village in one piece.

Second disciple: But Jesus said it would be OK. He must know people in the village. He must have arranged all this weeks ago.

First disciple: Maybe. But I don't like it. Have you noticed how Jesus keeps trying to tell us that his life is in danger in Jerusalem. If he's right, going into Jerusalem with a stolen donkey doesn't seem to be a very good idea. What if its owners complain to someone. The Pharisees are looking for an excuse to arrest Jesus. This could be it.

Second disciple: I don't think so. I think this has all been arranged. Jesus knows what he's doing. Come on, we're nearly there.

Narrator:	The disciples found the donkey tied to the wall; and as they untied it, its owners asked them what they were doing, and they told them that Jesus needed it, and the owners understood.
First owner:	They came then, like Jesus said they would.
Second owner:	They did. One of them looked really scared. I think he thought I was going to hit him.
First owner:	And they took the donkey.
Second owner:	They did.
First owner:	Jesus should be all right with that donkey. He's young, and hasn't been ridden before, but he's strong and inquisitive. He'll be fine.
Second owner:	Jesus riding on our donkey into Jerusalem – that'll be a story to tell the grandchildren.
First owner:	But he's taking a risk, going into Jerusalem, he knows that. The Pharisees will be watching him.
Second owner:	They will, and they'll be watching our donkey as well.
Narrator:	The disciples took the donkey back to Jesus, and they put their cloaks on the donkey's back and helped Jesus onto the donkey, and Jesus began to ride into Jerusalem.
First Pharisee:	Have we got everything in place?
Second Pharisee:	We have our people watching all the entrances into Jerusalem.
First Pharisee:	We know Jesus will try to enter Jerusalem today. We can't stop him, he's too popular with the crowds: we don't want a riot.
Second Pharisee:	But we need to know what he's saying. We need to find an excuse to arrest him, and we need to do that quietly when

there are not many people around. Today is not the day to take him.

First Pharisee: Today is the day to watch and listen. He can't escape us forever. We'll get him in the end.

Narrator: As Jesus and his disciples approached the road that led down from the Mount of Olives others joined them and a noisy crowd of people began to thank God loudly for all the things that they had seen Jesus do.

A child: Mum, mum, I can hear a noise. Is Jesus coming? Is he coming now?!

Mum, mum, John and Sarah have gone to the other gate of the city to see Pilate, who is going to be riding a big, big horse. Do you think Jesus will be riding a big horse too?

The shouting, mum, it's getting louder. Are they coming?

I've got a huge branch, mum – it's bigger than the branch John and Sarah took with them. Can I wave it, mum? Can I wave it now? I'll be careful.

Narrator: As they walked along behind Jesus into Jerusalem, the disciples shouted and praised God. They shouted:

Disciples, child, owners of donkey, stones: God bless the King who comes in God's name.

Narrator: They shouted:

Disciples, child, owners of donkey, stones: Peace in heaven, and glory in the highest heaven.

Narrator: And some people waved branches they had cut in the fields, and others laid their cloaks on the stony road.

A child: I saw him, mum, I saw him. I squeezed through people's legs and got to the front. I had to leave my branch behind, but I picked it up after he'd gone.

He wasn't riding a big horse mum, he was riding a donkey. But he looked great, and everyone was shouting and smiling. Lots of people put their cloaks on the road for the donkey to tread on. Red cloaks, blue ones, green and yellow ones. The road looked amazing.

And I shouted mum. I shouted: 'God bless Jesus! God bless the king!' And Jesus saw me, mum, and he smiled at me. It was great.

Wait till I tell John and Sarah about this – who cares about Pilate and his big, big horse. I bet they haven't had so much fun as me.

I'm hungry now, mum. Did we bring anything to eat?

First Pharisee: King, they're calling him a king! I've had enough of this! Who does he think he is?

Second Pharisee: We can't do anything now, there are too many people around.

First Pharisee: We may not be able to do anything but I'm going to let him know we're here!

Second Pharisee: There's too much noise. He won't be able to hear you.

First Pharisee: He will. Jesus, teacher – tell your disciples to be quiet. Tell them to be quiet now!

Narrator: And Jesus heard what the Pharisee said and he replied:

Jesus: If my disciples keep quiet, the stones around us will shout out loud.

First stone: Did you hear him?

Second stone: Pardon?

First stone: Did you hear what Jesus just said?

Second stone: I can't hear anything – someone's dumped a green and yellow coat on top of me!

First stone: He said if the disciples stopped cheering, us stones will shout out loud!

Second stone: Don't be silly, you can't have heard it right – you've got a fleecy tartan jacket around your ears.

First stone: But he did.

Second stone: I'm sure he didn't. If we shout out loud people will know that we can think and talk. They're not supposed to know that, and anyway I've never spoken loud enough for people to hear me, and neither have you. I don't know if we could.

First stone: But if Jesus tells us to shout we'll be able to, won't we. Wow! This is really exciting.

Narrator: As Jesus came closer into the centre of the city he began to weep:

Jesus: O Jerusalem, if you could only recognise the things that make for peace. But today, you cannot see it. There will come a time of war, when your enemies will set up barricades around you and surround you on every side. Then they will destroy you, you and all the people within your walls. They will not leave one stone upon another.

Narrator: And after this Jesus and his disciples went further into Jerusalem towards the temple.

And the Pharisees followed him.

And one small *boy/girl* and *his/her* mother went home.

And the stones slept.

Ruth Burgess, Spill the Beans

Mum, I'm hungry (a script for two voices)

Mum, I'm hungry ... Mum, I'm hungry and I'm bored ... Mum, why are we standing here?

I'm not sure why we're here, Chamor. I think we're waiting for someone to fetch us.

Well, I wish they'd hurry up! I'm bored ... Mum.

Yes, Chamor.

Look there's two men people coming. Listen, mum, they're talking to our owner.

Chamor, we are going with these men – you need to stay close by me and do as you are told.

Yes, mum, I will. I promise. Where are we going, mum?

Chamor, I don't know.

Mum, where are we?

We're getting near Jerusalem, Chamor, and it's a very busy place. Stay close.

Yes, mum.

Mum, why are these men putting coats on your back? Look, mum, they've put a coat on my back too – it's tickly.

Mum, is someone going to ride on you? Is someone going to ride on me as well?

I don't think anyone is going to ride on you, Chamor, you're too small to carry anyone yet.

Mum, he's a nice man, that man on your back. He smiled at me and scratched me behind the ears. He's kind.

Chamor, there are lots of people here. I think we're going to move in a minute. Make sure you stay very close.

Yes, mum.

Wow, mum it's really busy and there's people everywhere. And we're walking on people's cloaks and there's branches all over the road. Is this Jerusalem, mum? It's so noisy. Everyone seems to be shouting. And they keep looking at us. Mum, I'm scared.

Stay close, Chamor, and you'll be all right. I don't know who this man is but people seem to like him. With him on my back I know we'll be safe.

Mum, I'm being good, aren't I, mum?

Yes, Chamor, you're being very good.

Mum. Where are we? Why have we stopped?

We're in Jerusalem, Chamor. That's the temple over there. I've been here before.

Where's the kind man gone, mum?

He's gone into the temple, Chamor, with some of his friends.

Wow, mum, look – there's people running out of the temple. Mum, they look really cross. And, mum, there's pigeons all over the place. Where have they come from? They're making an awful mess. I hope the kind man is all right, mum. I liked him. He was nice.

Mum.

Yes, Chamor.

Mum, I'm really tired now and I'm ever so hungry.

We'll be fed soon, Chamor. And then I think someone will come to take us home.

It's been a really exciting day hasn't it, mum?

Yes, Chamor, it's been a day that we won't forget.

Ruth Burgess, Spill the Beans

Are you coming?

A: What on earth happened to you?!

B: Oh, I'm having the most incredible day! You should come along!

A: Look at the state of your cloak! How did it get so mockit *(filthy)*?

B: It's the donkey. You know Jesus is pure brilliant!

A: Donkey?! Where on earth have you been? That looks like hoof-prints!

B: Yup. The donkey's been walking on it! Lots of times. It's fabulous!

A: What? You let a donkey walk all over you?

B: No, no, I took my cloak off and spread it out in front of Jesus. Everyone's doing it! All the way down the road! It's like rolling out a red carpet (except we haven't invented red carpets yet).

A: Could you not have found an old cloak that's already falling to bits, if you want to let a donkey tramp all over it?

B: I've only got this one cloak, the only one I've had for years, as you well know.

A: Exactly. And you need it to last another few years, and you need it in one piece, to keep you warm at night. You're lucky you've only got a couple of wee tears. People like us can't afford new cloaks whenever we get daft notions about donkeys.

B: We're doing it for Jesus! Have you ever met anyone like him?! We have to show everyone that he's the man! The Pharisees are telling him to shush us up, but he puts them in their place! He's the best.

A: You're making a right royal fuss of Jesus right under the Pharisees' noses? Do you want to be arrested?

B: If you don't want trouble you should be across the city with Pontius Pilate, throwing your cloak on the road for him, showing a bit of respect for the Emperor.

A: Nobody respects the Emperor – or Pontius Pilate! Parading into the city as if he owns the place, as if he can do what he wants, as if we all love him. What a joke!

B: That's just it! I think Jesus is laughing at him today, poking fun at him. He's never let us make a fuss of him before, but on the very day Pilate is riding round town in all his pomp and ceremony, Jesus is having a party on a donkey, with all of us going crazy for him, singing and shouting. Glory to God! Woooo hooooo! Are you coming?

A: Can we *all* come?

B: *(to everyone)* Bring your coats! Come and tell Jesus he's the best!

A: Let's go!

Follow on with whatever kind of procession is possible, inviting everyone to throw their coats and jackets down to make a trail around the worship space. You could sing a song as people process.

Jo Love, Spill the Beans

If our Queen rode a donkey

Lord Jesus,
if our Queen rode a donkey
for her Jubilee
we would laugh.

If the Prime Minister
rode a donkey into Parliament
we would laugh.

If Simon Cowell
rode a donkey to *Britain's Got Talent*
we would laugh.

But with you it is different.
May we, like you,
put aside power
and show love instead.

May we, like you,
put aside pomp
and show and meet people
where they really are.

May we, like you,
put aside fortune and show the world
the kind of love you have:
humble,
human,
real,
without glitz.

May we meet you there.

Roddy Hamilton, Spill the Beans

Let us journey with you

Holy, Holy, Holy God,
great is your name.
We want to shout it from the rooftops,
we want to sing it from the balcony,
we want to share it with everyone.
You are our God, and we are your people.
Hosanna, hosanna,
hosanna in the highest.

God, we want to praise you today;
we want to shout and sing,
to celebrate the coming of Jesus to Jerusalem.
We are happy and want to share it
with everyone who will listen.
We don't want to look too far ahead,
into the week that is coming;
we want to stay here, happy and content,
celebrating your presence.

Holy God, stay with us today,
enjoy this time of worship,
hear our songs and prayers,
fill us with love,
send us out ready to face the future.

Don't let us be afraid,
don't let us shy away from the pain,
don't let us rush to Easter,
but let us journey with you in the coming days.

Spill the Beans

A blessing of palm crosses

We thank you, Lord, for these palm crosses,
a simple reminder of the love you showed for us.
As we take them into our homes,
may they remind us through this special week
that you gave your life for us upon the cross.
May they remind us of how deep and wide and high
is the love you have for us.
As we take them into our homes,
so may we take your love into our hearts
and worship you as Saviour and King.
And like the people on that first Palm Sunday,
may we also cry, 'Hosanna,
blessed is he who comes in the name of the Lord!'

Simon Taylor

Palm Sunday Evening

We see the crowds

Tune: 'Mary Morrison' (Scottish traditional)

We see the crowds that called you king,
and wave our hands, and cry with them,
convinced with them you come to bring
the kingdom to Jerusalem.
We see a throne raised over all
and by it, we in glory shine –
not hearing you in Pilate's hall:
the name you use is yours, not mine;
the word is yours, not mine.

We see you kneel to weary friends
and wash their dirty feet for them,
and still believe that, in the end,
it leads towards a diadem.
When Pilate nails a taunting sign
above the man he crucified
we grasp at that, and leave behind
what all your actions signified,
so plainly signified.

O Christ, you know how human minds
crave dominance and majesty,
and will not see the countless signs
that say you choose humility.
Christ, help us not to join the crowd
that chose Barabbas over you;
to turn our backs on high and proud
and always serve as you would do,
and serve as you would do.

Roddy Cowie

See: https://audioboom.com/posts/6057912-palm-sunday

After the palms and the parade

After the palms and the parade,
after the shouting and the shoving,
after the Hosannas and the hopefulness,
we find ourselves following you through inequality and unrest,
a world full of violence and brokenness,
and we worry about what we can do.
At least we can pray for this world and the people in it …
and we can pray for those who lay down their lives …
and we can pray for those who lead us …
We are here to follow you.
Give us strength for the next step.

Silence

After the palms and the parade,
after the shouting and the shoving,
after the Hosannas and the hopefulness,
we find ourselves following you through disease and mortality,
a world full of struggle and despair,
and we worry about what we can do.
At least we can pray for those without jobs or homes or friends …
and we can pray for those who are ill or infirm …
and we can pray for those who mourn …
We are here to follow you.
Give us strength for the next step.

Silence

After the palms and the parade,
after the shouting and the shoving,
after the Hosannas and the hopefulness,
we find ourselves following you through apathy and hostility,
a world full of anger and mistrust –
and more than a little of it is our fault –
and we worry about what we can do.
But we know we need to pray for ourselves,

called to be your holy Church ...
We are here to follow you.
Give us strength for the next step.

Silence

After the palms and the parade,
after the shouting and the shoving,
after the Hosannas and the hopefulness,
we realise we are following you into trouble,
following you to empty ourselves and die for the world,
even as you emptied yourself and died for us.
Give us the strength to follow,
out into the world,
out into daily life,
into pain and death
and what you have shown us comes beyond death.
Give us strength, hear our prayers,
even as your Son, our Saviour, gave us words to pray:

Our Father ...

James Hart Brumm

A child's-eye view

1. Palm Sunday

'Look, they're coming!' someone shouted.

There were crowds of people everywhere. They were standing at the sides of Jerusalem Road, and everyone was cheering. Some were breaking pieces off the palm trees nearby – are you *allowed* to do that? – and waving them like flags. Others had thrown cloaks and palm branches onto the road like a carpet.

I tried to wriggle my way to the front of the crowd but people's elbows kept getting in my way. I couldn't see anything, so my dad lifted me onto his shoulders. That was much better! There was a man riding a donkey. I guessed he was a king, the emperor, or a Roman soldier who had just won a battle.

'Who is he?' I asked.

'Jesus,' mum answered. 'He comes from a place called Nazareth.'

The cheers got louder and louder as Jesus and his friends came nearer. People were shouting 'Hosanna, Hosanna, God bless the one who comes in the name of the Lord' as they waved their palm branches. I wasn't sure what the word 'Hosanna' meant but I joined in anyway.

Mum told me everyone hoped Jesus was the person God had sent to save us – I think she meant from having to pay so much money to the Roman government. That would be really good.

Jesus had a kind face. He gave me a special smile when he saw me sitting on my dad's shoulders and heard me cheering loudly. I think Jesus must like children.

2. In the Temple

The next day we went to the Temple. My brother and I were playing some singing games with other children while we waited for mum and dad to make a sacrifice.

Suddenly, we saw Jesus and his friends come into the Temple. 'Look,' I said, 'it's the man on the donkey – the man we saw yesterday!'

But something had changed. Jesus wasn't smiling any more. He looked very cross. He went to the place where some men where exchanging money and suddenly threw the tables onto their sides. Coins rolled everywhere. Then Jesus went to the place where people were selling birds for the sacrifices and opened all the cages. Jesus shouted something about the Temple being his Father's house and that what the men were doing there was wrong. 'It's a place where people should pray,' he said. 'It's not a street market.'

Pigeons and doves were flying everywhere. Feathers were flying through the air and we ran to collect as many as we could. There was bird poo all over the special floor. It was so funny! We tried hard not to giggle. It was going to take someone a long time to clean up all that mess! The Temple priests were furious.

They were even more angry when they saw Jesus talking to the people who had come to ask if he could make them better. Lots of them could not walk and others could not see. We watched – amazed – as Jesus made them well. They were laughing and singing and dancing. We thought Jesus must be a very special person if he could do things like that.

We pretended to wave palm branches in the air and sang 'Hosanna, Hosanna' – just like we had done yesterday. The priests glared at us but Jesus heard us and gave us a really big smile.

I told you he liked children!

Kathy Crawford

Let's stay with the Hosannas

Let's stay with the Hosannas for a while.
Let's let them keep on ringing in our ears.
Hosanna!
Blessed is He who comes in the name of the Lord.

Instead of rushing on to hear the cries
that came later in the week,
let's stay with the Hosannas.
Maybe once we've heard those in a new way
we will be ready to make the rest of the journey:
a journey that was given new purpose
for those Hosannas were not simply
the innocent cries of palm-branch-waving children.
Those Hosannas were the war cries of adults,
tired of the oppression of occupying forces.
Those Hosannas were the hopeful cries
of a nation seeking liberation.
Those Hosannas were an investment of hope
in one they believed would deliver.
Those Hosannas that we have sanitised over the years
rang out in clear insurrection,
sealing the fate of one who rode on a donkey.

So, let's stay with the Hosannas.
Let's wrest them from the lips of children
and allow them to sound from our mouths
and ring in our ears
as a call to action,
a call to justice,
a call to love.

Let's stay with the Hosannas
even as we journey with the Christ,
who carried those Hosannas all the way to the cross
and ensured their fulfilment as the justice and love of God.

Liz Crumlish, Spill the Beans

Jesus needs his friends (a sending)

There is a tradition that sees the whole of Holy Week as one long service and so no benediction is pronounced.

The time is not yet,
but the darkness is gathering.

The time is not yet,
but the main players
are taking their positions.

Dither not,
but come back tomorrow
and wait with the Son of God,
for his friends are few
in this world of hatred.

The time is not yet,
but our time is now:
to be here
and trust a love
that will see this thing through.

Go,
but be back,
for Jesus needs his friends.

Roddy Hamilton, Spill the Beans

Monday, Tuesday and Wednesday of Holy Week

Three liturgies

Monday in Holy Week

Opening responses:

Your love, God, reaches to the heavens.
Your faithfulness touches the clouds.

Your righteousness is as high as the mountains.
Your justice is as deep as the seas.

How precious is your faithful love.
In you we find shelter and light.

Reflection on John 12:1–11:

They knew.

Who better to understand than this family
who had already tasted death.
Who better to understand than these sisters and their brother
who had always loved him.

When Jesus came to their house in Bethany
they knew,
and they got dinner ready for him.

And Lazarus sat at the table with him,
and Martha served the meal,
and Mary poured perfume all over his feet.

And Judas, who was there too, asked a question:
'Why wasn't this perfume sold
and the money given to the poor?'
And Jesus answered him:
'Mary poured this ointment over my feet
because she knows what is going to happen to me.
I won't always be here, Judas;
the poor people will always be with you.'

And outside the crowds gathered,
and the chief priests heard what had happened
and they planned to kill Lazarus as well as Jesus.

And in the house of the family who understood
the fragrance of the perfume lingered.

Closing blessing:

Go now and walk with Jesus towards Jerusalem.
Listen to his words,
be with him on his journey.
Let his story linger in your house and in your life
and let him welcome you.
And may God bless you,
the Maker
the Son
and the Holy Spirit.
This night and all your nights and days.
Amen

Liturgical action: *use nard/spikenard perfume to mark a cross on people's hands.*

Intercessions: *those who offer hospitality, hospices, people who are dying, and those who love and support them …*

Tuesday in Holy Week

Opening responses:

A: Strong as a rock,
safe as a castle on a crag
is the love of God our maker.

B: Powerful as a story,
bright as a light in the darkness
is the love of Jesus our Redeemer.

C: Wild as the wind,
tender as a loving parent
is the love of God the Holy Spirit.

Reflection on John 12:20–36:

Narrator: Jerusalem was crowded.
The streets were busy.
People had come in from the country,
even from other countries,
for the Passover festival.

In the midst of the crowds was Jesus, and with him his disciples.

Those who were near enough to him could hear what he was saying.
Those further back caught snatches of his words.

Listen.

A: He's talking about seeds
and how a seed only grows
when it's buried in the earth.
B: He's talked about seeds before –
he told a really good story about a sower.
A: But this is different;
it sounds more like a story about death and burial.

C: He's talking about eternal life.
D: He said once that loving your neighbour and yourself
and loving God with everything you've got was the way to eternal life.
C: I remember that.
He's saying now that anyone who loves their life in this world will lose it.
D: I wonder what he means by that.
C: Maybe he's going to say more.

A: He's talking about death again.
He seems to be praying.
Something about an hour and glory

B: Wow!
Was that thunder?
What a rumble!

A: Someone's saying that the thunder was an angel
speaking to Jesus.

B: An angel? Wow! What kind of an angel makes a noise like that?

C: He's talking about judgement now
and the Son of Man and the Messiah.

D: People have asked him before if he's the Messiah.

C: He's saying that he's going to be lifted up and everyone is going to be able to see what's happening to him.

A: He's telling us to walk in the light
because soon it's going to be dark.
He says if you walk in the dark
you don't know where you're going.

B: That's true enough – I can understand that.

A: He's telling us if light is in us we'll be people of light.

B: I remember he told us that we shouldn't hide our light, that the light in us must shine so that people will see good things in us and give God glory. That made sense to me. I've never forgotten it.

D: What's he saying now?

C: I don't know. He seems to have disappeared.

Narrator: Jerusalem was crowded.
The streets were busy.
People had come in from the country,
even from other countries,
for the Passover festival.

In the midst of the crowds was Jesus, and with him his disciples.

Closing blessing:

Go now and walk with Jesus on the streets of Jerusalem.
Listen to his words,
be with him on his journey.
Let his light and love shine in you and around you
and let him challenge you.
And may God bless you,
the Maker
the Son
and the Holy Spirit,
this night
and all your nights and days.
Amen

Liturgical action: *give out seeds, or seed potatoes, which are traditionally planted on Good Friday.*

Intercessions: *farmers, gardeners, neighbours, travellers, pilgrims …*

Wednesday in Holy Week

Opening responses:

In light and love and laughter
God is with us.

In darkness and pain and betrayal
God is with us.

God knows through experience
What human life is like.

Reflection on John 13:21–30:

He came right out and said it –
'One of you is going to betray me.'

We looked at each other.
Who did he mean?

Did we dare ask him?
Could we bear to know the answer?
John was sitting next to Jesus
and Peter mouthed to him:
Ask him who he means?

John nodded
and edged nearer to Jesus
and whispered to him,
'Who is it, master?'
And Jesus answered him,
'I'll dip some bread in the sauce
and give it to him.
He's the man.'

We didn't hear what Jesus had said to John,
but we watched Jesus dip some bread into the sauce
and give it to Judas Iscariot.

Judas took the bread
and we all heard Jesus say to him,
'Go and do quickly
what you're going to do.'

Bartholomew wondered if Jesus was telling Judas,
who kept our common purse,
to go and give some money to the poor.
Philip remembered that in Bethany Jesus had told Judas
that poor people would always need help.
James thought that Jesus had asked Judas to go and buy
the things that we would need for the festival.

And while we sat and wondered,
Judas went out into the darkness.
It was night.

Closing blessing:

Go now and walk with Jesus into Jerusalem.
Listen to his words,
be with him on his journey.
Let his words question you and give you courage.
Let him change you.
And may God bless you,
the Maker
the Son
and the Holy Spirit,
this night
and all your nights and days.
Amen

Liturgical action: *in small groups share pitta bread and sweet and savoury dips, and share how you react to the characters in this story.*

Intercessions: *those who share our meals, those who live in places of danger, those who hurt others, those who are angry or sad …*

Ruth Burgess

Originally written for *Expository Times*

Remember her, remember me

(Tune: 'Love unknown')

I listened to his words
as twilight turned to night.
And suddenly I saw
a world transformed by light.
The light of love
that from him shone,
I realised too
would soon be gone.

I knew what I must do
and quietly slipped away.
I found the jar of spice
kept for a special day.
In talk-filled room
before them all,
I came to him
with offering small.

The perfume filled the place;
I combed it through his hair.
It did not matter now,
I showed how much I cared.
I wiped his feet,
my actions slow;
to him, alone,
my life I owe.

He took my hands in his
and I beheld his face;
beyond all words, I felt
my gift received with grace.
'Remember her,
remember me,
our deeds of love,
in years to be.'

Avis Palmer

Extravagant love (John 12:1–8)

Extravagant love does not care
what veiled betrayers and onlookers think.

Extravagant love looses her hair,
kneels at the feet of her beloved
and massages his feet
with the costliest lotion.

Extravagant love does not care
what veiled betrayers and onlookers think.

And what about us?
Where are we in this scene?
Do we kneel at the feet of the beloved
and wipe away cream with our hair?

Or are we the veiled betrayer
whose crimes are not yet revealed?
Veiled by a selfish, philanthropic act
which mocks the selfless love of our Lord.

Extravagant love does not care
what veiled betrayers and onlookers think.

Yet we stand embarrassed at extravagant acts
and cringe as we pass the street preacher.
And writhe with discomfort
at modern-day Marys who
kneel to anoint the feet of the beggar.

Extravagant love does not care
what veiled betrayers and onlookers think.

Extravagant love overflowed from the cross,
poured into our hearts by the Spirit.
Extravagant love anoints us to kneel

to wash our Lord's feet
and the feet of the outcast and sinner.

Lord, fill our hearts with extravagant love
that no longer cares
what veiled betrayers and onlookers think.

S Anne Lawson

What a waste

For two voices

What a waste – spending all that money on taking children to the seaside. You may call them deprived, but if their parents – presuming that they have any – got out and did some work, then they wouldn't have to rely on charity.

What a joy – to see the excitement, the amazement, the happiness, the shining faces of children who have never been outside the city before and never dreamed that they would ever see the sea.

What a waste – going to all that expense with flowers and shrubs and trees and a lake and ornamental statues. What good will it do? Who needs parks and gardens? Surely the money could have been put to better use than that.

What a joy – to find such an oasis of green and be able to exercise or stroll in the fresh air and take in the scent of the flowers. So many people have no space for a garden of their own. This area is a wonderful place for all to enjoy.

What a waste – to spend all that money on an elaborate Christmas party for those old people. Hiring a hall, putting on a full-scale meal, buying crackers, party hats, balloons, decorations and even bringing in a Father Christmas to give out presents – all far too much. Surely the money could have been better spent on delivering Meals on Wheels on a regular basis – letting people stay in their own homes instead of having to make the effort to go out.

What a joy – to see so many lonely people coming together to have a party. Some of them have no means of getting out of the house on their own and can go for days without seeing another person. Many of them get very few Christmas cards and no presents, because they have outlived their friends and have no close family. It is a delight to see them enjoying themselves for a change.

'What a waste,' said Judas, as Mary poured perfume over the feet of Jesus and dried them with her hair. 'How useful that money could have been if we had used it to feed the poor.'

'What a joy,' said Jesus, 'that someone cared enough for me to want to give me such an extravagant gift. The love shown by this gesture will help to carry me through the dark days ahead. Such generosity will never be forgotten.'

And in all acts of selfless generosity and compassionate love, the perfume of that moment lingers on.

Marjorie Dobson

Come Monday, Tuesday, Wednesday

Come Monday

Jesus groaned
getting out of bed,
trying to stretch out
the stiffness and tenderness
from riding that donkey;

hungry enough
to eat a donkey,
he grumbled under his
breath
when the service
was so lousy at
his usual eating place;

wanting to find
some silence and solace
he wandered into

church,
and wailed with grief
when he saw
that it had become
so upmarket
that those
who needed it
most
were not to be found;

come Monday ...

Come Tuesday

the Morally Superior
store
was back in business,
selling conspiracies
(buy 1, get 1 free),
fear (one size fills all),
and a variety of nails,
3 for a shekel;

people stood around
with their hearts
in their pockets,
listening to stories
again
and,
as usual,
missing the punchline;

stubborn-souled Jesus
gently,
softly,
hopefully
reminded folk
(once again)

that it is all about
relationships,
not rules, regulations, rituals;

come Tuesday …

Come Wednesday

the world stunk
with the bitterness
of intrigue;
the foul breath
of secret machinations
fogged the alleys
and byways
of the city,
while the silent
walls echoed
with
the whispers
of the lovers
of shadows;

the spines of the scolds
stiffened
and dander filled
their mouths
as they took umbrage
with the one
who spread solace
on the soul
of her Beloved,
when they
would have doused him
with the sour perfume
of self-righteousness;

come Wednesday …

Thom M Shuman

Well done, Judas

Someone sits in the middle of the worship space while one or two people walk round the chair, reading these words:

It has come to our notice, Judas,
that you are not entirely satisfied
with the state of play of your Messianic pretender.

We were just wondering, Judas, if we could help you in any way.
I think you know what we mean.
You see, we know, you know, your Messiah hasn't delivered freedom.
Heavens, we would all like to be free of the state.
Our oppressors would probably like to be free of us.
We both want the same thing.
But I think, and I think you think it too:
Jesus has not turned out to be that Messiah.

You're not very happy, Judas,
and like you, we're wondering how it all went so wrong.
Jesus seems to have pulled you in an unexpected direction.
There is not going to be any salvation here.
You're a Zealot and you've found yourself in the pocket of a pacifist.
Does that not make you look a fool?
Maybe we could help you?

Think about it, Judas.

Let us know.

We won't be going far.

We have Passover to celebrate.

You call us.

Pause

What?

Already?
You are impulsive!
A passionate fellow!

Well, I'm glad you came to us.
Judas, like we were saying,
we were thinking Jesus has turned out to be a bit of a disappointment.
But, maybe he's waiting for you.
Maybe his plan relies on you, one of his followers, Judas,
to recognise him and encourage him to make his move.

Maybe your Rabbi is just waiting for you to open the door,
to place him on the board where he can play that move,
to place him in the centre of the game, among the oppressors,
where he can call down the angel armies to free him and us.

If he is arrested then he'd have to do something.
He'd have to call on the Lord
to begin the battle and free us all.

It's a great vision, Judas.
And maybe, Judas –
you are the one called to make that move!

Have you been wrestling, Judas?

Have you been having nightmares?

Maybe it's a sign!
Maybe this is your time to bring things to a head,
to focus your man, to force his hand?
And what if you missed this opportunity, Judas, for Jesus?
What if you let this moment go by, when all of heaven is relying on you?

The voices are never clear, Judas.
You have to recognise the clues,
listen to those who know – like us, Judas.
We see the signs, so we wish to help,
to make it possible for you.

It could all be done in a flash, tonight even.
Just think, Judas, you would go down in history:
a holy man, a supreme example.

So, Judas, we were thinking,
all it would take would be a time and a place.

It would be such a relief to you –
all that anxiety gone,
those sleepless nights finished,
and all for a positive result,
one you were ordained to fulfil.

So, Judas, what do you think? …

You've already thought?

Thank you, Judas, thank you.

We want to say how grateful we are to you.

It is just a matter of waiting now.
Everything is in place …

But it is too late to change your mind, Judas.

You have done well.
You have made the right decision.
It's up to God now.

Oh, and, Judas, don't leave this behind.

Throw coins into the centre and freeze. Then leave.

Roddy Hamilton, Spill the Beans

Maundy Thursday

All is set

All is set. Following his instructions, we've rented a room, arranged the purvey. It'll just be Jesus and us – a good lads' night. What a blast we had the last time we did as he told us: borrowing that donkey, parading into town, men, women and children cheering us on.

It's been a funny few days: crazy laughter on the Sunday; temper tantrum on the Monday; telling it how it is on the Tuesday; beautiful woman with exquisite ointment on the Wednesday. I don't know what exactly he's got planned for tonight. One thing we can say for sure – it will be different: with him it always is.

We're going to rest up because this week's gone like lightning. Jesus has been like someone possessed. I'm sure that's why he organised the room just for the lads: some down time before whatever campaign he's got planned next.

He needs to keep a low profile anyway. He's upset a lot of folk this week. Bad enough parading into town like a king – albeit a king on a donkey – but then to turn the tables in the temple, literally, then tell more of his hard-hitting parables, and let himself be anointed semi-publicly when he knows that the authorities are watching and waiting for the chance to bring him down. They have to bide their time and choose their moment so they don't upset the people. Though even the people are turning: the palm-branch-wavers have already moved on to the next big news story, and you know how crowds can be when the mood turns ugly.

So we're making the most of this lull; gathering our strength so that we can support him through whatever happens. We're all he has left, the only ones he can rely on. The arrangements are made and so we rest.

Liz Crumlish, Spill the Beans

Come Thursday

Come Thursday

the powers that be
were being themselves,
lining up lackeys
to do their dirty work;
taking money
from petty cash
to pay a bribe
under the table;

Jesus was up early
working out his frustrations
as he kneaded the bread,
letting the grace
rise to a double measure;

decanting the wine,
he giggled
as the rich bouquet
of hope (with just a hint
of promise)
filled the room;

shaking the wrinkles
out of the tablecloth
(cross-stitched
with the names of all
who had eaten with him
over the years),
he spread it over
the scarred table;

now everything was ready;

come Thursday …

Thom M Shuman

Here we are

Here we are, O God,
gathered around your Table,
gathered together by your love,
all done trying to shift the blame away.
We know we betray you, every day,
but we are ready to try again.
Help us to follow faithfully.
Lead us, Christ our Master.

Here we are, O God,
gathered around your Table,
fed by your own body and blood,
re-calling you into our presence.
As your life fills us,
we feel the challenge to let you shine through us every day.
Help us live both holy and whole.
Fill us, Spirit of Shalom.

Here we are, O God,
gathered around your Table,
washed and dressed by your grace,
ready to follow you into the world.
We see the danger and death out in the world.
Help us to see you at work among us.
Fit us for our journey, God our Maker.

Here we are, O God,
gathered around your Table,
knowing there are crosses to be carried,
knowing there is Good News to be lived.

Triune God, ever leading us, filling us, fitting us,
strengthen us to walk with you:
for only by walking with you to the Cross
can we step into the glory of your Resurrection.

James Hart Brumm

Feet

Funny,
functional things,
feet.
As body parts go,
hardly the most attractive.
Bearing signs
of heavy usage –
dry skin,
toenails with sock-fluff,
bunions, corns, verrucas.
Often the innocent victims
of torturous footwear.
And the scent
is not always appealing!

Miraculous,
marvellous things,
feet.
Feet
take us dancing,
twirling, swirling,
swooping, gliding,
hopping, skipping,
jumping to the beat;
they carry us
to new and familiar destinations
where adventures wait.
Faithful feet,
steadily rhythmic,
taken for granted,
always there.

Feet.
Surely they deserve a little TLC.

Jesus,
you knew about feet.
Dusty feet,
hot feet,
tired feet,
foot etiquette.
But when you knelt
with the bowl and towel that night
(the night before your death),
tenderly cleansing those gnarled
grotty fishermen's feet,
it was more than TLC.

You took the part of a slave,
humbled yourself to dust,
and right there on the ground,
at foot-level,
you showed us
what love
and God
is all about.

And then you invited us to do the same.

Funny and functional,
miraculous and marvellous things,
feet.

Louise Gough

Foot washing – three takes

Peter

There is no way I'm going to let him wash my feet. Jesus is way too good for that. Way too good to go anywhere near my gnarled toes and cracked heels; and though I hate to confess it, especially at mealtime, I'm sure there's still fish scales stuck under my nails.

No way – not Jesus. Not my feet. Never. It's enough to put me off my dinner.

But he's washing Andrew's. And he's washing James's. And no disrespect, but their feet aren't exactly a pretty sight – or smell – either.

He doesn't seem to mind though. It's almost reverential, the way he's touching those feet. It's as though he's washing the feet of Moses, or Elijah, or his beloved mum; he's being so gentle, so tender. This is way beyond the kind of wash most hosts offer – a swill in a bucket, a rough towel, wipe your hands and grab a glass of wine. This is hospitality plus. Jesus is taking his time; he's paying attention to what he's doing. He's listening to each of us in turn; it's as though this really matters. No – this isn't ordinary hospitality. This is something else, something different. Something poignant. There's love – and there's sorrow – in his eyes.

What's that, Jesus? ... Unless you wash me, I can't share in your ministry? O Jesus – wash me, then – wash my feet, my hands, my head – wash all of me! Douse me in your goodness. Make me clean, and fill me with love. Make me fit to follow you – because I'd do anything for you.

Judas

He knew. From the moment he washed my feet – so undignified, there on the floor. A teacher should be washed – he shouldn't be the one washing feet. Even now, his crazy ideas still infuriate me. What equality is this? Servants greater than their masters? Is he trying to start a revolution?

But he knew. Because he said one of us wasn't clean. I could barely look him in the eye as he washed and dried my feet; I tried not to squirm. But he understood – he even gave me a cop-out – he said this would be done to fulfil scripture, that I'd been chosen just for this.

Then he told me to go. So after he'd given me the bread, I slipped out. And believe me, I wasn't on a mission to buy some extra food or give to the poor. I slipped out to set in motion his death.

Jesus

They have no idea how much I love them – and how much I want them to love one another. Tonight, I couldn't have made it clearer. Things are closing in on me; my time is coming, the hour of my suffering is here. Soon I will be gone; gone to the Father. I'm depending on them to continue what I've started, what we've started. Other than what waits for me tomorrow, I couldn't think of a better way to sum up all I've tried to teach them except by washing their feet – because to minister you have to be the least; it's the only way to raise up the humble and bring down the proud. I am not relishing all that lies ahead, but I know it is the will of God, and my suffering will be his glory. They will not recognise it at first – most of them won't even be there (they'll have scarpered) – but tomorrow I will stretch myself to show them the extent of God's love, the depths of it. In all these things, I am giving them a new commandment, and a new challenge before I leave them: to love one another as I love them; to love with the bowl and the towel and the cross, so that others will see their love and know that they are my disciples. When people look at my followers, I want them to see me.

Louise Gough

A night of wonder (John 13:1–17)

I look back on that night with wonder.

Jesus was so confident in who he was and how much God loved him. All the stuff he told us, all those words that were later remembered and cherished and written down: how he was the vine and we were the branches; how he was the way and the truth and the life; how the Holy Spirit would always be with us; how he prayed for us; how God loved us.

But before all that, there was the business with the towel and the bowl of water; it was so strange.

He went to Andrew first. Andrew was so surprised that he did as Jesus asked him.

Andrew took off his sandals and Jesus took hold of one of Andrew's feet, poured water over it and washed it. Then he did the same with the other foot. Andrew sat there, stunned, his feet dripping water into the bowl that Jesus had placed on the floor. Then Jesus took the towel that he had tied round his waist and gently rubbed Andrew's feet dry.

Bartholomew was next. The same treatment. The water and then the towel.

Nobody spoke a word.

It soon became clear that Jesus intended to wash all our feet, opting out was not an option. Thomas next, and James and John and Matthew.

And then he approached Peter – and Peter exploded. No way was Jesus going to wash his feet! No way was Peter going to let Jesus do something that should have been done by a servant.

But Jesus told him that unless his feet were washed he would not be able to be a disciple, and Peter announced that in that case Jesus had better wash his hands and head as well.

We all laughed. Even Judas, who had seemed a bit cross recently.

Jesus told Peter and the rest of us that for that night washing our feet was enough. Later we would understand what this foot-washing was all about.

I smiled at Jesus when he came to wash my feet. He looked so serious, almost sad. And he was so gentle. I remembered my mother washing my feet when I was a child. It tickled. It felt good. The towel by now was damp, but he was still able to rub my feet dry.

When Jesus had gone round everyone, he took his place again at the table. He talked to us about what he had done. He told us that we were all clean, except that one of us wasn't. We were puzzled at that.

Then he told us that we were right to call him teacher: he was our teacher, our rabbi. And because he had washed our feet, we should wash each other's feet. None of us was to feel ourselves more important than the others.

I am glad that we wrote down what we remembered of that night. I've never forgotten it. I remember it when I wash my children's feet, or my grand-parent's. I remember it when I meet with Jesus' friends.

I look back on that night with wonder and I always will.

Ruth Burgess

Let you wash my feet! (John 13:1–15)

Let you wash my feet!
How can I?
They are soiled with all the dirt and mess of the road.
Besides, such an intimate act.
I am afraid, so I keep running,
rushing through the days packed with encounters and meetings;
filled with words, sadly not always filled with the Word.

'Let me wash your feet,' you say.
Calling but not insisting, for that is not your way.
When at last I am compelled by exhaustion to sit down,
there is the bowl, the towel and you.

There is nowhere else to go.
So taking my courage in both hands
I plunge my feet in the water.
So cool, so refreshing.
My feet are soothed, and not just my feet –
the whole of my being is filled with
your presence.
And I wonder yet again why it took me so long
to let you wash my feet.

Elizabeth Clark

Here is a table

Call to worship:

Here is a table around which a story is told; not anyone's story, but everyone's story: a story that makes no sense and holds no hope, unless we dare to believe this is not all there is. For in the background, in the shadows that disturb the street below, whispers are passed that speak of betrayal: of this being the night of rulers and anti-rulers conspiring with the darkness to break the man of light; of religion's leaders and empire builders and puppet kings working together to crush the dream of hope; of followers confused, being possessed by fear, willing to deny, and too tired to care.

But as the world turns to trap him, Jesus does one more thing that opens God's love to be shared evermore: he breaks bread and sips wine, and as the darkness builds around him the light of this story casts its brilliance down the centuries and bathes this table tonight for those who dare believe …

Reflection:

On the communion table are twelve unlit candles. As each name is said a candle is lit. Twelve people could come from the congregation to do this.

This is the story that holds every story, mingled here with the stories of people whom Jesus met: all those he touched, everyone he brought back into community.

You: the woman at the well who drank that living water.

A candle is lit.

You: Zacchaeus the tree-climber who broke the mould of tax collectors.

A candle is lit.

You: Jairus' daughter who rose from sleep and knew new life.

A candle is lit.

You: Peter who chose to have his feet washed, and then denied Jesus three times.

A candle is lit.

You: Lazarus who fashioned the way of resurrection.

A candle is lit.

You: Mary for whom Jesus could find no accusers.

A candle is lit.

You: the Syro-Phoenician woman who challenged Jesus with an inclusive kingdom.

A candle is lit.

You: Andrew who found a picnic and thought it might become a feast.

A candle is lit.

You: Martha the worker with no time to rest and listen.

A candle is lit.

You: the haemorrhaging woman who dared reach out and touch the hem of his garment.

A candle is lit.

You: when you deny me and hurt me and do all kinds of things to me.

A candle is lit.

You: Judas betrayer who tried to force the hand of the kingdom.

A candle is lit.

For each one, Jesus broke bread and said, 'This kingdom is for you.'

For each one, Jesus shared wine and said, 'The promise is alive in you.'

For each one, Jesus requested, 'Make this the one thing you always do to remember me.'

Prayer of approach:

Lord Jesus,
as the light thins and the world conspires,
may we tell your story.
When hope seems gone and the future broken,
may we tell your story.
When the hungry need fed and injustice is rife,
may we tell your story.

Yet may we tell it not just in this place
but in every place,
for this story is the hope of the world:
this bread, the means of a new world,
this wine, the promise for all,
this table, a meeting place for terrorist and terrorised,
for warmonger and peacemaker.
May we tell this story
which plants hope and sows longing
into the fabric of the world.

So we come as we are, O Lord Jesus,
with all the worry we have,
the ability to change sides so easily,
the fear of the future
and the hurt of the past,
with what is broken in us
and what is a burden to us.
We come as we are,
with all that we have done.

May we trust the symbol of this table and the story it tells:
renew us;
refocus our vision;
dare us to believe;
call us anew and name us your body in the world.

Lord Jesus, as the light thins and the night thickens,
may we be here,
because there is no other place to be,
and may we remember you.
Amen

Setting the Table:

After each voice, a goblet of wine or bread is placed on the table.

As we hear the voices of people whom Jesus met, we set the table.

Voice 1: I met him at a well, this border-crosser who spoke to me when no one else did. 'Give me a drink,' this Jew said, and this Samaritan almost did, but my thirst was deeper, and he knew.

Place goblet of wine on table.

Voice 2: He wanted to wash my feet. I said 'No!' He looked at me in that way he had that told me I had missed the point. I still don't understand but I let him wash my feet anyway.

Place bread on table.

Voice 3: He drew a line in the sand for me and for them, one none of us dared cross: 'Who will cast the first stone?' he asked without looking up. And finally, when he did look up, my accusers were gone, for love had crossed the line.

Place wine on table.

Voice 4: He called my name, but not with mourning in his voice. 'Lazarus!' he called. I heard him and I walked towards him.

Place bread on table.

Voice 5: He did not want them to go hungry, neither did I. Five loaves and two fish were never going to be enough. The miracle happened – and small offerings became a feast of vision as bread was broken and shared.

Place wine on table.

Voice 6: No one calls me a foreign dog and gets away with it, and neither did he. You saw it in his eyes – it struck a chord. 'Even the dogs eat the crumbs,' I said, and heaven suddenly got larger in his mind and we foreigners were included.

Place bread on table.

Institution:

For each of the people Jesus met, and for us gathered here, Jesus says:

'I love you; you are part of the kingdom's story.
Your stories come together here
in bread and wine and the Table of redemption,
and tonight of all nights
make this the one thing you do together:
Remember me.'

Song: 'Put peace into each other's hands' (CH4 659)

Pause

Communion prayer:

Lord Jesus,
we pause at this table
because all the stories have been told.

Pause

Promise seems so fragile now, hope seems much thinner.
We cannot find the words we need, the questions are too great.
All we have is silence.

Pause

Yet here we no longer need words.
The kingdom is breaking, love is choosing, the darkness is conspiring
and we find ourselves here because
there is no other place to be and nothing else to say.
We can only break bread and share wine and be with you tonight.

Pause

So may we use the only words left,
the angels' song,
that we might believe through this night:

Holy, holy, holy Lord,
God of power and might,
heaven and earth are crammed with your glory.
Hosanna in every nook and cranny.
Blessed is the one who owns God's name,
hosanna in the highest.

Come, Lord Jesus,
break the bread for us,
pour the wine for us,
this word in flesh
is all we need.
So be it.
Amen

Ending:

In many traditions, on Maundy Thursday, there is no benediction. The congregation simply leave in silence. The deed is done, Jesus is betrayed, and now arrested. There is no coffee or fellowship, just the loneliness of the night.

The following words may help shape that departing. The lights of the church are dimmed or switched off completely.

And when they had supped,
the betrayer having already left,
they went out into the night.
In the dark
the trees seemed to twist around them
and whispers filled the night across the city;
adults talked,
babies cried,
but the garden was still.
And as Jesus prayed on his own
the followers left him and fell asleep.

Blow out one of the candles after each of the following lines:

You: the woman at the well.
You: Zacchaeus tree-climber.
You: Jairus' daughter.

Can you not stay awake with me?

You: Peter denier.
You: Lazarus unbound one.
You: Mary set free.

Take this cup from me.

You: Syro-Phoenician woman.
You: Andrew the disciple.
You: Martha the worker.

Can you not remain here with me?

You: the disciples today.
You: when you deny me, hurt me, forget me.
Ah, Judas, you have come back.
Judas?!

Blow out final candle.

Silence as people leave.

Roddy Hamilton, Spill the Beans

Peter's story

A monologue written for Holy Week Communion Service. To be spoken after Communion, initially standing at the Communion table and then moving around the church.

Time's a funny thing when ye tak the breid and the wine:
the 'then' and the 'noo' and the 'no yet' a' slidin' intae wan anither.
The Maister tellt us that every time we took breid an' wine
we were to mind him.
Mind! I'm no likely to forget in a hurry.
O Peter, Peter! ye were aye wan for openin' yer big mooth
and pittin' yer fute in it
but ye fairly coo'd the cuddie that time …

Peter – that was the Maister's name for me.
My mither and faither ca'd me Simon.
Simon! What kind o' a swanky name's that for a fisherman's laddie?
Oh, I ken it could hae been waur.
Left to himsel', my faither wad hae ca'd me Nicodemus!
But Simon … I've never liked the name.
I mind sayin' as much to the Maister when I first met him.
'Weel,' he says, 'we'll jist hae to think o' anither name for ye.
What wad ye like me to ca' ye?'
'Oh,' says I, 'I've aye fancied the name Rocky –
that's a braw name for a laddie.'
He looked at me –
he had a wye o' lookin' at ye that seemed to go richt through ye,
almost as if he kent ye better nor what ye ken yersel.
'Na, na,' he says, 'I dinnae think so.
Rocky's the fantoosh word they use doon sooth
when they mean 'shoogly', ye ken.
An' there's nothin' shoogly aboot you.
Leal, aefauld and straicht-backit, that's you,' he says.
'Leal, aefauld and straicht-backit.'
I thocht he was puin' my leg.

'Me?' I says. 'Och, I'm jist a big saft tattie. The ither laddies used to cry me Simon the Saftie.'
'No adaursay,' he says, 'there's granite in ye, lad, granite.
And that gies me an idea. I'll jist ca' ye Peter –
it means "granite" ye ken.'
And whiles eftir that,
when I'd left the fishin' an' was gaun aboot wi' him and the ithers,
he'd come ower the same thing again.
'Ye can aye lippen to Peter,' he'd say.
'Leal, aefauld and straicht-backit. There's granite in him, granite.'
And yet he must hae kent what wad happen –
it wisnae cannie hoo he aye seemed to ken
what was gaun to happen before it did.

He kent onywey what wad happen if he went doon sooth
but richt reason or nane, naething wad dae him but to gan.
It was the unco guid:
he'd fairly put their birse up, and they wantit him dune awa' wi'.
The unco guid ... ye ken the kind,
mim-mou'd, ticht lippit, faces like soor plooms,
aye runnin' to the kirk,
aye girnin', aye flytin', aye greetin' aboot something,
and aye thinkin' they're the bee's knees,
the 'chosen anes'.
As my auld granny used to say, 'Self-pride cam' stinkin' ben.'
But it wasnae their self-pride in itsel' that stuck in the Maister's craw.
Eftir a', there have aye been folk, and nae doot aye will be folk,
that cannae think they're worth onything
unless they're lookin' doon their noses at a' the rest o' us.
It was mair what their self-pride made God oot to be,
wee, and faur awa' and pernickety,
pickin' on this yin here and that yin there to be guid tae,
and giein' a' body else the nippy sweetie.
But shairly ... shairly, gin God be God,
he's bound to be big, and near,
and hae room in his hert for onybody that wants,
even for a common five-eighth like masel.

Ye can see I've been wi' the Maister!
He wad say that if onybody, onybody at a',
taks a tummle tae themsels and wants tae win back hame to him,
dae ye no think that God wad hing oot the flags when he hears that they're comin',
and run to meet them when he sees them at the road end?
What faither wadna dae the same?
And that was why the Maister was sae deid set on gaun sooth.
He thocht if he got the ear o' the heid bummers doon there,
he micht save them frae themsels an' start changin' things.
He was aye a gambler, the Maister,
aye ready to tak' a chance on folk.
But gaun doon sooth was a chance that was nae chance …

We could a' see that, an' he kent it fine an' a'.
At that last meal we shared thegither, he turns to us and says,
'The Shepherd'll be felled, and the sheep'll be skailed.'
'Me?' I says. 'I'll no be skailed.'
Me and my big mooth.
'I'll gan wi' ye a' the wye – to the jyle, to the death if need be.'
He looked at me. 'Eh, Simon, Simon,' he says.
Simon! He hadna' ca'd me that a' the time I'd been wi' him.
'Eh, Simon, Simon,' he says. And he didna seem roosed,
jist kinda vexed ye ken.
'I'm tellin' ye, lad, afore the cock craws the morns mornin'
ye'll hae threepit ower and ower again that ye dinnae ken me.'
I thocht that maybe for aince he'd got it wrang,
but before I could say ony mair
he said somethin' I couldnae understaund at the time.
He says, 'When ye come back to me,
pit some o' that granite o' yours into your brithers.'
And then we a' went oot.

What happened eftir that is a' a bit o' a jummle.
I mind o' a gairden, and torches, and shoutin', and a bit o' a collieshangie,
and a' body runnin' awa' except me.

They took the Maister to a kind o' a coort buildin', and I followed on ahint
(had I no said I'd gan wi' him a' the wey?).
At the coort I slippit in to a wee waitin' room place.
Ye could hear the voices up the stairs whaur they were tryin' him.
It was a cauld nicht, and I cooried doon at the fire to try and get warm.
A lassie comes ower to redd up the ash,
and she says something aboot the weather.
'Yes,' says I, 'it is gey cold the night.'
I thocht I was daein' a' richt at the pan loaf.
But she says, 'Ohh,' in that twistit wey they speak doon sooth.
'Oh,' and their mooth gans a' agley, 'don't you speak funny.'
Me speak funny?
'You're from the norf by the sound of it,' she says.
'Wait a minute – that's like him upstairs. Are you a pal of his then?'
'What way do you think I'm a pal of his, lassie?' I says.
'I have never even met the man.'
'Gaun,' she says. 'You give yourself away every time you open your mouf.
And come to think of it, didn't I see you wiv him
when they brought him in just now?'
'How dovie can you get,' I says. 'I am telling you I do not ken the man.'
There were some gairds sittin' there, an' wan o' them says,
'Come off it, mate.' An' then, tryin' to be funny:
'It's a braw brikt moonlikt nikt the nikt. You're obviously from the north.
You lot are all the same – come down here and try to tell us what to do.
You must've come down with him.'
I was in sic a feery-farry by this time
that the pan loaf went oot o' the windae.
And I says: 'I've tellt you till I'm blue in the face
that I dinnae ken the man
and dinnae care what happens to him.'
Hardly were the words oot o' my mooth
when they brocht the Maister doon the stairs.
He never said eechy nor ochy, but he looked at me
and that fair ca'd the feet frae me.
I ran oot into the close, greetin' like a bairn.
The gairds must've thocht I was some kind o' a safty
for they never even came eftir me.

It was dark that nicht, the darkness o' Genesis,
but the nicht oot there was nae blacker than the nicht in here.

The corrie whaur the deid shaddies fa' …
It seemed like the end o' everything.
The Maister's life wasted, and a' for what?
And I'd let him doon.
'There's granite in ye, lad, granite …'
Aye, right.
Peter? It was mair like bein' petrified – turned to stane.
That's what it felt like – a deid wecht inside.
I went back to the fishin' – it was a' I kent.
But that didnae work either.
We never caught onything.
The nets were aye empty, just like my ain hert.
When I looked into mysel' I could find nothin' livin',
nothin' the spirit could feed on.
And then, wan mornin', when we brocht the boat in,
there he was, standin' by the side o' the loch.
We didnae ken wha' it was at first
but we heard him cryin' to us to let doon oor nets wan mair time.
It's a guid job we did, for when we brocht them up again,
they were that fu' o' fish that they were like to brek.
My hert was like to brek an' a', for I kent then it was him.
The next thing I'm ower the side o' the boat into the watter,
and then I'm runnin' like a whittrock to whaur he was.
That face …
Gude kens whaur he'd been, or what he'd seen,
but the face had nae licht in it,
like a hoose blacked oot, wi' a' the blinds doon.
'Simon,' he says. Simon again!
'Simon,' he says. 'Dae ye love me?'
'Aye, Maister,' I says, 'I dae that.'
'Simon,' he says again. 'Dae ye love me?'
'Aye, Maister,' says I. 'Ye ken I dae.'
It was as if he hadna heard me. 'Simon,' he says again. 'Dae ye love me?'

'Maister,' I says, 'ye ken a' that's in my hert,
and ye ken the place that there is in my hert for you.'
'Ah weel,' he says, 'Peter' –
and the licht had come back into his face –
'I've a job for ye, Peter.
Ye'll look eftir my sheep, Peter, and ye'll feed my wee lambs.
And mind, noo, Peter, the door o' the sheepfauld's aye to be open,
it's never to be steekit,
so that ony o' my sheep that want back in at ony time can get in
like what ye've jist dune yersel.'
So that's what I'm daein' noo – herdin' sheep.
I dinnae ken what kind o' job I'll mak o'd.
But when somebody believes in ye like that,
when they ken no just a' ye are,
but a' ye could be,
ye feel the least ye can dae is try and live up to what they see in ye.

(Move back to the communion table)

Aye, time's a funny thing when ye tak' the breid and the wine,
the 'then' and the 'noo' and the 'no yet' are a' gathered up into wan,
like draps o' rain runnin' doon yer windae.
When I tak the breid and the wine thae days,
I dinnae jist look back: I look forrit an' a'.
When ye've been to the lip o' the corrie whaur the deid shaddies fa',
it begins to dawn on ye that there's a faur side to the corrie
an' ye begin to think o' what micht be waitin' for ye there.
The Faither's hoose?
A table spread and plenished wi' guid things?
The Land o' the Leal?
But wan thing I'm shair o': the Maister'll be there.
And that'll dae me just braw.

James Munro

Radical

It is a week that begins so well. The crowds roar their delight as he rides into town – Word is on the street. He is teaching, healing, and the crowds surround him.

Mid-week, the mood turns along with the tables in the Temple. Not good for business, all this chasing folk from stalls, making whips from cords, berating them for just earning a living, running about as if he owned the place. These country folk don't understand the art of tact and diplomacy. Hackles on backs are raised while there are still some who seek a miracle. His friends are getting twitchy watching as he dances dangerously on the edge. Wary, they walk the city trying to keep a low profile, keeping their heads down and wishing that he would do the same. He doesn't play the game: speaks out against the powers that be for not caring for the least, for loving privilege more than these.

On Thursday, his friends are fractious, cracking under stress. He bids a couple to go prepare a meal. Over bread and wine and blessing, he talks of his body breaking and bleeding, wants them to eat the bread and drink from his cup of suffering. It's all too much – and they lash out at one another: fingers point and accusations fly. They fight for top position on what is feeling like a sinking ship. His words, though quiet, cut through the conversation: overturn their notions. He tells them of God's kin-dom, built on loving service: seeing, hearing those ignored and those unheard, and making space at the table for all. Radical. That kind of talk will get him killed.

Spill the Beans

Judas reflects

It wasn't the money ... of course that helped. But it was more of a bonus than anything else. You don't get something for nothing any more.

I work with money so I know its value. Thirty pieces of silver isn't to be sneezed at.

But it wasn't the money ...

You see, I always knew. That it would be me. It had to be me.

Peter, he's too soft. Thomas, too indecisive. James, too much of a hothead. But me, I always stayed on the sidelines. Tried to be objective. Tried to gauge what was happening. Tried not to get too caught up in it all. It was my job. It was my duty ...

It's not that I didn't believe what he said. All that talk of love and kingdoms to come. I believed him. Or at least I wanted to.

He had the gift of the gab – and more. No mistaking. But he went about it the wrong way. His approach, it was too haphazard, too disorganised. There was no planning. You need a plan if you're going to get anywhere in this world.

All he did was rub everyone the wrong way, and that is dangerous. He went looking for trouble, and that's just irresponsible. We've got enough to worry about without drawing attention to ourselves. I didn't want to be a part of that ...

I just can't understand him. He had the perfect opportunity: charisma, pulling power, and something else. I don't know what. But there was something about him, and he could have, we could have, used that to get what we all wanted. That's why I did it. Because it was all going pear-shaped and he needed to be brought into line. Not stopped. Just reminded about who was in charge and that he couldn't go around shouting his mouth off, winding people up, putting us all at risk with his outrageous God talk ...

When I kissed him, I could taste the wine on his lips. I looked him in the eye, so he'd know that it was for the best. It was a relief to see him smile. He needed a 'get out' and I'd given it to him. I knew then. I knew that's what he'd expected of me all along. I should have done it sooner and saved everyone a lot of grief. It's what he wanted …

Was it my fault? If it hadn't been me, it would have been one of you. I may have turned him in, but he wasn't exactly invisible, was he? They'd have got him in the end. And the crowds … that was the justification, as if I needed any. Yes, he was my friend, so were the others. But they were too caught up in it to see the implications.

It had to be me. It wasn't the money. It was my job. It was my duty.

Tina Kemp, Spill the Beans

Gethsemane

We should have been there for him

We sensed it might be the last Passover meal we would ever share together.

Jesus must have known that too, and so he wanted to make it a memorable occasion for us.

He certainly succeeded!

First of all, Jesus took a towel and wrapped it around his waist. Then he filled a bowl with water and started to wash our feet. That was a servant's job. Jesus was our master. It seemed wrong, and I told him so. But Jesus insisted, so I let him.

The meal was really enjoyable, until Jesus started to talk about sacrifice. And then Judas spoiled everything by walking out. If we had known why, some of us would have stopped him. I suspect Jesus realised.

At the end of the meal we went outside and began to walk across the Kidron Valley. There was a garden there that we often went to. A gentle breeze was stirring the olive trees, but it was a clear night and stars were shining brightly. We sang a hymn as we walked.

Jesus moved a short distance away from us and began to pray, as he often did.

Some of us sat down and closed our eyes for a few minutes. We must have nodded off. It had been a busy day – or maybe we had drunk too much wine!

Jesus woke us up. He was clearly distressed. 'Couldn't you have stayed awake?' he asked.

We should have been there for him but we were too tired. We saw torches and lanterns in the distance, and heard lots of people walking towards us. Then we noticed Judas go up to Jesus and greet him – obviously a pre-arranged signal to the soldiers and Temple police with him. How could he do that?

I could never betray Jesus like Judas did. I'd brought a sword in case of trouble and I wasn't afraid to use it. I lashed out. Someone got his ear chopped off.

Jesus was arrested and taken away. I was surprised they didn't arrest me too. I was becoming really scared.

John insisted we should be there for Jesus, so we followed at a distance. He knew the High Priest, so we were allowed into the courtyard of his house. The girl at the gate spoke to me. She must have recognised my Galilean accent. 'Are you one of that man's followers?' she asked. 'No,' I answered.

The soldiers had lit a charcoal fire to keep themselves warm. I went to stand near it.

'Aren't you one of Jesus' followers?' someone asked.

'No, I'm not,' I replied.

Another man asked me, 'Didn't I see you in the garden with that man?'

'Definitely not,' I said.

Things were getting worse.

As dawn was breaking I heard a cock crow. Inconsolable, I wept.

Kathy Crawford

Watch with me

Lord,
I am not good at heroics.
I can't say that I would die for you,
because I don't know.
At least, not yet.

No.
I can only cradle you,
rock you as you sob scalding tears
against my shoulder.
I can only stroke your hair
and let my tears bathe your head.

I cannot say, 'There, there, everything will be all right.'
Because it won't.
I cannot say, 'I know, I know.'
Because I don't.

Will my tears ease the agony of the crown of thorns?
Will my embrace counter the stretch of tendons pinned out on wood?
I don't know.

All I know is that in watching with you
your anguish becomes mine,
and mine yours,
and as my tears mingle with yours,
my wounds with yours,
together we wear the wounds of the world,
and carry them into the night,
towards the impossible possibility
of resurrection.

Sr. Sandra Sears CSBC

At midnight in a garden

(Tune: 'Down by the Sally Gardens')

At midnight in a garden,
a man knelt down to pray.
The darkness gathered round him;
the silence on him lay.
And joy had turned to sorrow
and doubt must have its way,
when in a midnight garden
the Lord knelt down to pray.

At midnight in a garden,
some friends were waiting near
to keep watch and to guard him,

be with him facing fear.
But promises are shallow,
and tiredness turns to sleep,
when in a midnight garden
the Lord was heard to weep.

At night-time in a garden,
a man stared at his fate:
a coming day of horror,
a coming day of hate.
The day of crucifixion
when crowds will mock and jeer.
The cup of suffering's drunk from.
The day of Love is here.

At night-time to a garden,
the guards and elders came
to shackle and arrest him
for all his God-like claims.
And frightened men forsook him,
and friendship was deceit.
At night-tine in a garden,
a kiss was bitter sweet.

This night-time to a garden,
our thoughts and feelings go.
We watch, so deeply grateful,
the Lord we've come to know.
His love is undiminished.
His peace is ours today;
for in a midnight garden,
our Lord kneels down to pray.

Avis Palmer

In Gethsemane

The flower of all humanity
stretched out beneath the olive trees,
his eyes welled full of bitter tears
knowing what evil times drew near.

The mind that danced with birds and seas
and pierced the prophets' mysteries
knew surely what he had to choose –
his to accept, or to refuse.

The scourges, stripping flesh from bone;
the long drag to the killing stone;
the shoulders slowly ripped apart
leaving his weight to crush the heart.

And darkening the heart of pain
the knowledge he would cry in vain
while God soared on supreme on high
changeless and holy as he died.

The flower of all humanity
stretched out beneath the olive trees,
and chose the way he knew was right
and greeted Judas in the night.

Roddy Cowie

Take this cup away from me (Luke 22:42)

He thought we were all asleep – but I wasn't. Peter's snoring kept me awake, so I just lay there watching. It was a beautiful warm night, with a full moon shining overhead, and I felt totally at peace. We'd had a wonderful evening and I mulled it all over again as I lay dozing, seeing again that upper room, the table, all my friends – and in the middle the friend I loved more than words can express. Judas had been acting a bit strangely, but had left early, and the rest of us were in a blessed haze of warmth and comfort and expectation. Something miraculous was happening, or about to happen. Jesus held me in his arms and I lay against his chest listening to the steady thump of his heart, thinking I was in paradise.

Perhaps it was because I was so much younger than the rest that he was so kind to me. I don't know – all I know is that I absolutely adored him, worshipped the ground he walked on, didn't ever want to be parted from him. I'd always known I wasn't like other boys. I was at the age where I should have been getting interested in girls, but somehow it wasn't happening and I knew it was something I had to keep to myself. It wasn't that I didn't like girls – I had four sisters and I loved them dearly; I had no objection to playing with them and they were very protective of me. I just couldn't picture myself getting married. My father had a girl in mind for me and was starting to make noises about a betrothal; the idea terrified me but I knew I would have to go through with it. He would have killed me if he'd known how I really felt.

Jesus was simply the most magnetic person I had ever met. He came through the village one day and I went along to hear him speak – I'd never experienced anything like it, and without a thought I went and spoke to him and asked if I could join his company. There was a bit of muttering from Peter and the rest because of my age, but some of the women piped up and said they would keep an eye on me, and the others agreed.

It became something of a joke that I was his favourite, but it wasn't a joke to me. He was very careful not to single anyone out – it was just that I think I understood him a bit more than the others. They were so slow, so preoccupied with themselves and their own ambitions; sometimes I wondered whether they could really see him at all. It was obvious to me that he wasn't talking about some huge military conquest. I sensed his unease as we came towards Jerusalem, and yet the rest were still talking about armies and King David and the overthrow of the Romans. I could feel his sadness and loneliness at their incomprehension – he kept on saying that he was going to die, but they just didn't want to hear it. As for me, I tried not to think about it; I knew what was going to happen but I couldn't bear the idea, so we never spoke about it. He knew that I knew though.

Sometimes we would sit together for ages, not talking – we didn't need to talk – staring into the fire; or he would put his arms round me and we'd just stay like that, our hearts and minds united. I was one of the very few people he allowed that close to him; Mary of Magdala was another. As we got closer to the city he seemed to need our company more, and I sensed his fear.

Until that night, however, nothing awful had happened – in fact it had been wonderful. The cheering crowds, the triumph and excitement – I began to wonder if my premonitions had been wrong, if we really *were* on the brink of some glorious revolution. The atmosphere in the city was wild and I could feel something gathering to an enormous crescendo – it would only be a matter of days. We were all completely high as we rollicked into Gethsemane – not drunk, but totally intoxicated with anticipation and happiness. We'd been there many times before, it was a favourite spot, and we settled down happily under the trees to catch some sleep. Tomorrow, I thought … tomorrow something will happen. I gazed at the stars, listening to the others' breathing slow down and become deep and regular as, one by one, they fell asleep.

Jesus wasn't asleep though. From where I lay I could see him; the moonlight shone on his face as he leaned against a big old olive tree, looking up at the heavens. I watched as he stood up and crept quietly away, careful not to wake anyone, grass and branches rustling under his feet and the cool wind ruffling his hair.

Perhaps I dozed for a while too. All I remember is that I suddenly felt a terrible chill, and opened my eyes with a start. The wind had changed and it was cold; I shivered and pulled my cloak round me, snuggling into its folds. Around me the others mumbled and snuffled, deep in sleep. I had a sudden moment of panic – where was Jesus? Had he left us? But no – he was standing a few yards away, looking down at his slumbering companions. But his face – his face! I had never seen him look like that before. He was chalk-white and his eyes were red; his features seemed blurred like a smudged painting, his cheeks blotched, his lips trembling. I was struck with terror at the sight – he seemed like a stranger, unmanned, disintegrating before my eyes.

'Peter! Andrew! Wake up!' he hissed. Nobody moved. I shut my eyes quickly, not wanting him to know I was watching. He bent down to Peter's bulk and shook him.

'Wake up! Please, wake up. Please, Peter, help me.'

But Peter's regular snores continued. I was astounded. I had never heard Jesus speak that way – he sounded like a frightened little boy. He always knew what to do, nothing scared him – not storms, not the anger of the elders, not disease or death – what was wrong with him?

He stood up and stumbled off into the darkness. My heart almost burst in my chest – I could hear him crying, a heartbroken desperate sobbing that seemed to shake the trees and rocks around us. Why could none of the others hear it? What could I do to comfort him? The pain in my heart was physical, and for some reason I couldn't get up. It was as if some great force held me down, and it was torment. I thought I was going to suffocate or die, and yet my limbs seemed paralysed and I couldn't even open my eyes. As I lay in agony, I heard the grass rustle and sensed him standing beside me. I felt him crouch down, felt his warmth, felt him shake my shoulder.

'John. Please, John. We have to leave. I can't do this. Come on, we have to run away – they're coming for me now.'

There was nothing in the world I wanted more than to jump up and throw my arms round him, run away with him, protect him from whatever was coming – but I couldn't move. He was crying and his hot tears dripped onto my face. They ran into my mouth and trickled into my hair, and still I lay like a stone. The wind howled around us and the moon had gone in; a blanket of darkness surrounded us, a darkness so profound that it seemed no light would ever penetrate it again. I felt him waiting for my response, watching me, hoping against hope – then I felt him get up and move away. Instantly I could move again. I opened my eyes and saw him kneel down in the grass and cover his face with his hands.

Sooty blackness swirled around us; it seemed as if it had a shape; I thought I saw it writhe and coil round his head, over his back, around his neck like a great serpent. With a groan he collapsed and lay there. I started up – was he dead? I had no idea what was happening to him or what he was thinking but his agony was clear and I ached to know how to help him. But before I could get up I sensed the blackness receding. The shadows seemed to slither away and I could see the stars again. A golden beam of moonlight suddenly broke through the clouds and bathed Jesus in its light, and I saw his body relax; he rolled over and his chest heaved as he breathed in the cool perfumed air of the garden. His face was calm, not the terrible ravaged mask of a few minutes before – he looked like my friend again, and relief surged through me. I jumped up and ran over to him; the others began to wake up with snorts and mumbles, stretching and yawning and rubbing stiff limbs.

I put out my hand to help him up and he grabbed it gratefully and sprang to his feet. He gripped my hand tightly; somehow I knew that he was aware of what I had seen, that I had been with him in his torment even though there was nothing I could do to relieve it. I wanted to tell him, to let him know how I had felt, but before I could say anything there was a loud noise, and Judas burst into the garden at the head of a gang of soldiers.

Had I but known it then, there was a still harder task waiting for me. To stand and watch him die in pain and humiliation, to be beside his mother in her heart-breaking vigil – I don't really know where I found the strength. Except perhaps during that awful night in the garden, when I was the only one allowed to be with him in his greatest weakness. When I lay down I was still a dreamy boy; when I got up I was a man, a man with power and vision and self-respect. Youngest of his followers perhaps, but not the least – entrusted by him with the care of his family and the telling of his story. Perhaps he did love me best after all.

Catherine Harkin

In the courtyard (John 18:12–27)

What a night! There were people everywhere. The courtyard was packed. Soldiers, servants, guards from the temple – there was very little room to turn.

I'd seen them going out earlier, the soldiers and their commanding officer; they were armed and carrying lanterns and torches. The man who they called Judas was with them; he looked haunted, almost scared. And for some reason Malcus, the high priest's slave, was with them, and some other slaves too. I have no idea why they were there.

They returned with a man who they must have arrested. He was bound. I glimpsed his face. It was the man they called Jesus. The teacher. Malcus stumbled into the courtyard; he looked stunned, something had obviously happened to him, but I had no chance to ask him what. Another man came in, who I knew; he'd been here before I think. There was no sign of Judas.

The man who I knew came over to me and asked if one of his friends could come into the courtyard and warm himself by the fire. It was a cold night. I didn't see a problem as with all those soldiers and guards milling round there was not likely to be any trouble. When he brought his friend in I thought I recognised him. I asked him, 'Aren't you one of the disciples that followed that man Jesus?' He said very quickly, 'No, I'm not.' Perhaps he was afraid of being arrested too.

They went and stood with the guards and servants and slaves keeping warm around the fire, which was in the middle of the courtyard.

Someone else asked the man again if he was a disciple of Jesus the teacher, and he denied it.

One of the slaves keeping warm by the fire was related to Malcus. There seemed to be a rumour going round the courtyard that a man called Peter had cut off Malcus' ear, but Malcus hadn't looked as if he was wounded, so I'm not sure if that was true.

This slave must have been with the soldiers because he asked the man if he'd been in the garden. Garden? Maybe he meant near the brook in Kidron: it wasn't far away. Again the man said, 'No,' and he said it very loudly.

And somewhere in the distance, we all heard a cockerel crow.

It was morning.

Ruth Burgess

Wine is poured and bread is broken (A hymn for Maundy Thursday)

(Metre: 8.8.8.8, suggested tune: 'Ae fond kiss', CH4 786)

Wine is poured and bread is broken;
new, portentous words are spoken.
Least that's said is soonest mended:
'Go, my friend, the meal is ended.'

Stars, they say, shone bright to greet me;
strangers travelled far to meet me;
moonbeams silently descending
tell the world my life is ending.

All that might have been and won't be;
all I hoped to see and won't see;
unborn children, roads untravelled;
hopes destroyed and plans unravelled.

Had I lived in isolation;
had I loved in moderation;
would I now have peace and plenty?
Would my cup be full or empty?

All alone in bleakest sorrow;
all alone I face tomorrow;
hungry flock, who now will feed you?
God, where are you when I need you?

How I long for dawn – and fear it;
will I have the strength to bear it?
Adulation turned to malice;
must I drink this bitter chalice?

Not yet conquered, death approaches;
not yet harrowed, hell encroaches;
as the founds of earth are shaken
God's own son is God-forsaken.

J Mary Henderson

Good Friday

Come Friday

Come Friday

palms were stuffed
into trash cans
for the post-Passover
pick-up;

nails
were strewn
in the path
of the
cross-bearer;

little kids
stopped their games
of street ball,
pressing their backs
against shadowed
walls
as death
came striding by,
arm in arm
with
Pilate and Herod;

and
the silence
from his friends
was deafening;

come Friday …

Thom M Shuman

Good Friday (an all-age service)

Opening responses:

On Good Friday
We gather together.

Old and young
We gather together.

To tell the story
We gather together.

We gather together in wonder.
We gather together in love.

Song

The story:

On the day we call Good Friday Jesus was put to death outside the walls of Jerusalem at a place called the Skull. His body was nailed to a cross by the soldiers. His friends and his enemies watched him die.

Reflection:

Jesus had enemies.
Jesus had always been watched by the people
who didn't like what he was doing.
Some people didn't like what Jesus said about God.
Some people didn't think he should heal people on the Sabbath day.
Some people didn't like the stories that Jesus told.
Some people weren't happy about who Jesus shared his meals with.
Some people didn't like what Jesus said about them.

Jesus had lots of enemies and he also had lots of friends.

The friends of Jesus liked what Jesus said about God.
Some people liked the stories that Jesus told.

Some people enjoyed having meals with Jesus
and talking to him about the things that they cared about.
Some people were grateful to Jesus for healing them
and healing their children.
Some people enjoyed asking Jesus questions.

The enemies of Jesus wanted to kill him; and when they got a chance, they told lies about Jesus and persuaded other people to join them.

The enemies of Jesus took him to the Roman authorities, and because Pilate, the governor of the province, was afraid that crowds of people might riot and cause trouble, he agreed that Jesus should be killed.

The friends of Jesus were very sad as they watched Jesus dying. It seemed that the enemies of Jesus had won.

Song

Introduction to action:

On Good Friday we remember the day that Jesus died. In a minute, when the music plays, you will be invited to look at things and do things at four tables around the church.

Table 1: Lots of people have drawn pictures of what happened on Good Friday or have made crosses of wood, pottery ...

So on this table there are pictures of crosses for you to look at and talk about, and crosses that you can look at, talk about and touch. You might want to take one of the crosses or pictures and sit down quietly for a minute and look at it carefully, and then take it back to the table so that other people can look at it too.

Table 2: On Good Friday we can remember the things that we have done to hurt other people and then say sorry to God.

On this table is a tray of sand. You are invited to think of someone you've hurt, and then to come and write the word Sorry in the sand. After you have done this, the person standing by the table will say to you that God forgives you and loves you, and will wipe away the word in the sand. Please don't come up close to the table until the person in front of you has moved away.

Table 3: On Good Friday we can remember the sad things that happen in the world and ask Jesus to be near to people who are in trouble.

On this table there is a map of the world. You are invited to think of a country where you know that people are sad, or in danger, or hungry, and to light a candle and place it on or near that country on the map.

Table 4: On Good Friday we can think about things we can do to make the world a better place.

There is a blackboard/white board on an easel, and lots of Post-its and pens on the table. You are invited to think of a way that you could make the world a better place for people and animals to live in, and to write this down or draw it on a Post-it and stick it on the board for everyone to see.

You are invited to visit the different tables. We will take our time. There is no rush. You may prefer to visit only one or two tables, or to stay sitting in your seat. You are invited to move when the music begins to play, and when the music has stopped you are invited to return to your seats.

Visiting the tables

Leader: One of the ways that Good Friday is marked in many countries is by the making and eating of hot cross buns. The bun is sweet and filled with currants or raisins and a cross is marked on the top.

After the closing responses, you are invited to come up to the front of the church to receive a bun and a blessing before you go home. (See Notes for the service.)

Song: 'May the God of peace go with us', CH4 786

Closing responses:

Old and young
We have gathered together.

Old and young
We have told the story.

We have told the story of what happened to Jesus.
We have told a story of love.

Buns and a blessing

Notes for the service:

Four tables to be set up around the church, which can be visited in any order by children and adults.

Table 1: A table with a range of different crosses and pictures of crosses for people to look at and handle, e.g. painted crosses, holding crosses, a crucifix, Celtic crosses … traditional and modern art.

Table 2: A large tray of wet sand on a table. A person to say 'God forgives you and loves you' and to smooth the word Sorry out of the sand. (A Post-it with the words 'God forgives you and loves you' should be visible to the sand-smoother.)

Table 3: A large map of the world laid on the table. Tea-lights supplied. People are invited to place a tea-light on the country they want to remember. (An adult and bucket of wet sand nearby in case of accidents.)

Table 4: A large black/white board with WE CAN MAKE THE WORLD A BETTER PLACE written on it. Post-its of different colours. Pens and felt pens. You might prefer to make a graffiti wall.

Buns and a blessing:

Depending on numbers and preference this can be done in different ways:

A: People could go to the front of the church individually. Someone hands them a hot cross bun. A person standing beside the bun-giver then puts a hand on their shoulder and says to them, 'God bless you and keep you' (or similar words). (Note: the bun-giver and the blessing-giver can be children or adults.)

B: A blessing could be given to the whole congregation and the buns distributed at the church door.

C: A blessing could be given to the whole congregation, who are then invited over to the church hall for tea, coffee, juice and hot cross buns.

Ruth Burgess

This is the day we dread

O Jesus
this is the day we dread.
It's a day
of breaking
of injustice
of sweat
of fear
of blood.

It's a day
of terror
of cruelty
of cowardice
of darkness
of death.

As we gather in this place
to worship you
we know that this journey
ends in crucifixion.

Today
when dreams to turn dust,
hope fades to despair
and love is drained,
reveal to us again
the cost of Godly-love,
and show us how to live it
amid the similar horrors
of our world.
Amen

Louise Gough

Hands of Jesus

A carpenter's hands,
work-worn and skilled,
shaping rough wood
with ease.

The hands of a friend,
open in welcome,
greeting all whom
he meets.

Hands of a healer,
with gentle touch,
caring for those
in need.

Hands of a servant,
with bowl and towel
washing the feet of
his friends.

Hands of my Saviour,
pierced with nails,
outstretched on a
rough-hewn cross.

Kathy Crawford

If God does not weep

Leave plenty of space between each stanza. You might use background music with this.

If God does not weep,
then there is no love deep enough
to touch the pain.

Pause

If God does not get close,
then there is no love real enough
to meet our brokenness.

Pause

If God does not touch,
then there is no love earthy enough
to value our humanness.

Pause

If God does not need compassion,
then there is no love tender enough
to endure our pain.

Pause

If God does not walk on,
then there is no love restless enough
to witness the truth.

Pause

If God is not anointed,
then there is no love ready enough
to die.

Pause

If God does not know pain,
then there is no love broken enough
to comfort our world.

Pause

If God does not know death,
then there is no love potent enough
to bring resurrection.

Roddy Hamilton, Spill the Beans

Who gets into paradise? (Luke 23:32–43)

Religious leaders have always been very clear on this one:
There are rules you have to keep and duties you have to perform,
and to have rules you have to have rulers – people in charge,
and the people in charge have to be very sure
that they are the right people to be in charge
and rewards and especially punishments are devised to keep people in line.

Who gets into paradise?
The ones who have ticked the boxes.
The ones who have earned it and deserve it of course!

And then there's this story,
the story that Luke tells of the crucifixion of Jesus,
with the religious leaders and the soldiers mocking Jesus
and the sign nailed above Jesus' head that read
'This is the King of the Jews'.

Luke tells us about a conversation between the two criminals
who were crucified with Jesus.

The first criminal hurled insults at Jesus:
'Aren't you the Messiah?
What kind of king are you?
Why don't you save yourself and us?'

The second criminal took him to task:
'Aren't you afraid of God?
We were all sentenced to be killed
and we're getting what we deserve for what we did.
We have been condemned justly
but this man Jesus has done nothing wrong.'

And then the second criminal turned to Jesus,
'Remember me, Jesus,' he said,
'when you come into your kingdom.'

And Jesus answered him,
'I promise you that today you will be in paradise with me.'

Who gets into paradise?
Only the ones who have ticked the boxes?
Only the ones who have been good and earned it and deserve it?

In dying, as in living, Jesus turns us
and our values
and our systems
upside down.

Ruth Burgess, Spill the Beans

The Red Road

All those years ago. No, I've never forgotten. Could never forget. But it is a story hidden away. Kept secret. They helped me at first, a woman watching with them through all those desperate hours, who went away weeping, shrouding her head, and then joining them in the first glad, crazy days of news and celebration. There were soon crowds of us. Crowds that I hid among, watching how the wind would turn, where the luck might fall for me. Always on the outside, watching, until who I was could be forgotten; and then like so many of them, I fled away to a new life, a new city and began again, and you find me after so many years. Now you come and stir those memories again, sharp as the edge of a knife. But it is right to tell you my story. It all comes together now, and must not be forgotten.

Always crowds, and always at the fringe. I can see it now, feel it even, in these hands that were once as light as butterflies. You'd never know, looking at them now, lumpen and twisted with age. Working the crowd. That's what we did. You could feel the tension in the hairs on the back of your neck – like eyes, I said they were, sensitive to every move and shift of what was going on. He would be at the edge, waiting to run on soles as soft as a cat, and I would take the purse, and gut it, catching the coins unclinking in my hand and getting them to him. Sometimes a bracelet, slit from a wrist, or a necklace. I was his woman. Yes, I know the names you would have called me. He never did.

We never knew any other kind of life. An alley in a back street, a rough childhood learning to dodge the blows, beg, scrounge, steal. If I hadn't met him, it would have been the streets for me, and the brutal handlings of a garrison town. But I met him, and we made a life, not love as you'd call it, but tender in its way and kind even, and a sort of home. A stinking rat hole in a back street, but the only place we knew where we could hide, and find enough love to survive and share what we could after the fence had taken his cut. We scraped by ... How old? I don't know. I don't remember much of my childhood. A woman who sang, sometimes, and drank other times, and shoved me out of sight behind a curtain when the soldiers came to her. As soon as I could stagger about I begged for her, and scavenged the rubbish in the Valley. I met him there, my Dismas, beggar like myself, but already sharp-eyed and quick to slide alongside a rich man and feel for the fat purse and slide his hand between the buckles. So I left my mother; left her, I remember with her head in a shawl, crooning, and the jug swinging empty from her hand. The pity of it, I know now.

We scraped by, I said. Just enough, and sometimes that bit extra for a drink and a hot meal at a tavern and a laugh and song with mates. That was how we learned about him. The crowds that gathered round him, and weaving through the crowd, people like us, begging or stealing or both as the people hung on his words. Sometimes they'd listen to him and come away generous with goodwill, and others, angry and proud, because he'd stirred them up, made them look at themselves and their religion. We had no time for religion, me and Dismas: it was only for the already good and the wealthy. If you were rich, God had blessed you. If you were poor, begging and thieving, scavenging on the rubbish, then somehow God must have no time for you. That's what we thought.

That's why, when I first caught the sound of his voice, it brought me up short. The ground was thick with people, from all over. You had the rough accents of the north, and the western voices from the coast around Tyre and Sidon, as well as the city voices, sharp as splinters, and the rich had to rub shoulders with the poor, with the farm workers and shepherds and women of the streets, and us. You could see them twitch themselves away, but it's hard to do so in a crowd with everyone pressing forward to hear him. So, just for a moment, I listened too and forgot to grope for purses and bags and trinkets. And he said, right out, 'Blessed are the poor … The hungry … the weeping ones … the ones who feel excluded. And woe to you, rich … and well-fed.' I can still remember it. It turned the world upside down for me, although of course we laughed about it that night, counting out what we'd stolen. What would he know about poverty and hunger? But what if it were true? Well, that began it, I suppose, for both of us, though I never realised it until much later.

We followed him, we had to, the pickings were too good, but with never the same ease of mind, like something uncomfortable pricking you like a thorn in the palm of your hand.

We were there in the crowd, me with my light fingers feeling the purses of the rich, the offerings of the righteous, and slitting them open silently, and my man at the edge waiting to vanish with the pickings; we were there, and he saw us. I knew that. Even as he began the story, his eyes moved around the crowd and saw us, and he told the story of the man on the road to Jericho, who fell among thieves, and the outsider who rescued him. He saw us, and knew us, and neither of us could quite forget it. Not fear. He wasn't going to denounce us. No, the kind of knowing that can get inside you, like water in a crack in a rock, and one day it will split you open. We knew the Jericho road: rich pickings if you were careful, but violence too, and some of it brutal. My man had done that, he and his partner: beaten up travellers and left them for dead. The Red Road, the Bloody Road we called it. If you travelled alone or at night, you were a fool.

Months later, it was, and all the city humming with the preparation for the Festival, and the rumours that folk like us could hear because our ears were always to the crack in the door, undercurrents of suspicion and hate and fear. The plans that were at work to trap and catch him, destroy him, that travelling preacher who dared to say that the poor were blessed, and who turned out the money changers in the Temple courts. All the city murmuring and throbbing and pilgrims travelling in from everywhere.

My man came back to me after two days away, tunic brown with blood. And blood that had gathered in the fine creases of his hands, sticky even then after hours hiding in the caves in the hills. So when he came home to me with his bloodied hands and hopeless eyes, I knew something had changed for him. Even now, I remember what he said and how his eyes fixed on me. 'I killed him. Slit his throat, the blood spouting out like a goat at a festival. No, not that little runt of a fellow in Jericho. The fat traitor that works in Bethany. He struggled. Called out when he felt the prick of the knife under his ear. So I killed him. It's not the first. But this one. This one sticks to me.' I brought water for him and washed his stained hands and took his tunic away to burn it, but we heard them clashing down the street, turning into the alley, jeering as they came. 'Come out, rat, we know who you are, where you hide. You were seen.' Even now, I remember the intake of breath, the horror and terror of the moment. We knew the punishment for theft and murder, especially the murder of a tax collector. The Roman law, in all its force, crashed in on us.

Two witnesses, a moment's trial, a flogging. They were eager to get the execution out of the way before the day of the Feast. They hauled him up. And alongside was his partner, angry and cursing that he had been caught, and that other man, that unforgettable preacher. What had he ever done to suffer this? I stayed with him, with the other women; and some of them I know now, and they helped me to survive afterwards.

We all heard the words spoken through that terrible day: the heat and then the darkness. The mockery, the courage, the long-drawn-out writhing pain of it. How do men think of these terrible things to do to one another? I heard his partner cursing, full of rage and fear and pain.

'Why don't you save us?' he sneered. 'You're supposed to be the Messiah. Well prove it!'

And I heard my Dismas answer him, 'Don't you have any respect for God? We're getting what we deserve for our crimes. But this man has done nothing wrong.' I watched him turn, twisting on those terrible nails and heaving himself forward to see this man, Jesus, and speak directly to him. 'Jesus,' he gasped. 'Jesus, remember me when you come into your kingdom.'

I saw them gaze at one another, two men utterly unlike each other yet now sharing an understanding so deep they could have been brothers. To speak, to turn and look, to hold that gaze was unbearable, yet they did so.

'I tell you the truth,' Jesus said to him, 'you and I will be together in paradise today.'

It was enough to hold him through the torture of the rest of those hours and the brutal mercy of the breaking of his legs so that he slumped forward and could no longer breathe. And I thought of him, with his friend, walking in the garden of paradise whilst we women washed the tormented bodies and prepared them for burial – I would not let them sling him into the Valley until I had washed and kissed his eyes and hands.

I have often thought of the story of the journey that Jesus told. And I realise that he was like them. Strung up like them, like a thief; and he was the one who fell among thieves, the victim, bloody and battered and his life stolen away; and he was the man riding to rescue us, the outsider, the one who got off his donkey to bind and bandage, pour in the stinging wine, the soothing oil. And I remember too, and it carried me through the days and weeks and months that followed, that he said: 'Blessed are those who weep. One day you will laugh again.'

That is my story, Dr Luke. You've found me here and heard me and you can see how my story and my man's story weaves in and out of those years when Jesus taught the people about mercy and justice, and then showed us exactly what he meant.

And afterwards? After that terrible day? I was taken in by one of the women, given a home. We were all sisters. They taught me how to sew and bake and I travelled with one of them as her maid and care for her now. She is very old, but her memory is still sharp, even of those days more than sixty years ago when she was a young girl. Wonderful stories. I know you have come all this way to see her. Let me go and see if she is strong enough to join you in the garden. I will bring drinks for you, and then leave you. These stories are precious to us women. Secret. But now it is time. It is time for them to be told.

Janet Killeen

The sister of Mary

I didn't want to be here you know.
Here, at the crucifixion; but I had to come
because of his mother, my sister.
I had to be here for her.
Jesus was the joy of her heart, the apple of her eye,
her firstborn – never mind how he was conceived –
firstborn are always special in a way,
and he was, mark my words, he was;
so good at following in his father's footsteps.
Then, after Joseph died, it all changed.
Oh he remained for a while as head of the household
but as soon as his brothers and sisters were able
to support their mother, he was off.
First of all he went to follow that wild cousin of his,
John (what a disappointment he must have been
to his elderly parents), the desert man,
living off locusts and wild honey,
just like one of those strange prophets, long ago.
But Jesus didn't stay long with him.
No, he came back up north and soon
had quite a following himself – a mixed bunch
from fishermen to tax collectors, the riff-raff
of society – with a few Zealots thrown in.
So it's little wonder he ended up here, really,
crucified between two criminals.
It shouldn't have happened though – he wasn't a rebel –
well, not in that sense of the word.
He was good and kind and healed people,
helped whoever came to him in need.
And now here he is, in need of us
as we lower his battered body, and rest it
in his mother's arms for one last time,
before we lay it in the borrowed tomb.
So that's why I'm in this place
where I really don't want to be, God knows.

I'm here for his mother, yet despite myself
I've become part of it too.

Carol Dixon

The worst of it

A monologue by Mary

The worst of it was not when he finally died.

After what they did to him, to see there was no more heaving of his chest, no more breath being gasped for, was a relief. His pain was over. They could not lay a hand on him any more. I longed to reach for him, to cut him down from there, to cradle him.

That was not the worst of it.

Seeing him exposed and broken, and being unable to hold him one last time, even in death. No mother should have to see her child tortured, mocked, insulted like he was. The way they treated him, like the lowest of criminals. Oh, my boy. But not once did he spit back or protest. Not even as he took the whip, as his skin broke and bled.

Even that was not the worst of it.

And the cruelty of crowning him with thorns, dressing him up like a king, parading him out in the streets, bowing and scraping around him, jeering and howling like crazed animals, enjoying their contempt for him. And I could not stop them. I could not stop any of it. I could not rescue my son. I could not even grasp his hand, speak a word of love in the chaos. I tried to keep as close as I could in all the pushing and shoving of men and soldiers, but I was powerless to ease his torment.

Even that was not the worst of it.

I could not look as they took the nails and ropes and forced him down then hoisted him up. I knew what to expect – we have all seen it before. The wretchedness of hanging there for days, waiting for the mercy of death. How long would it be for him? How long till he breathed his last? I feared it would be slow and long for him.

But that was not the worst of it.

No, the worst of it was his shout, his wail of abandonment. I do not know how he had the breath left for such a harrowing cry. He cried against heaven, against the Almighty, a final desolate groaning at being forsaken in the end. Forsaken by his Father. At the end of your faithful, passionate, joyful life, my son, in the end they defeated you.

Oh, my child. You were never cut off, forgotten, left by our God. You were never abandoned, even at the last! But you cried out the misery of being deserted, the pain overwhelming you in the end. Who can blame you? But after all your years of hope and faith, all you taught us, all your life and laughter, I cannot bear that at the end you felt cast aside by your Father, our Father. 'My God, my God, why have you forsaken me?'

Jesus, my boy, if only I could tell you, it was never like that. You were anything but forsaken! You were loved to the end, loved beyond death. Oh God, why did they break you so completely?

Why?

Jo Love, Spill the Beans

Blood and bone

My dad had green fingers.
Mum used to say that
he could grow lilies
in a rubbish dump.
'What's the secret?'
I asked him one day.
'Blood and bone,' he said,
'blood and bone,'
and tipped me a wink.

My Father is a gardener,
working in wasteland,
making deserts flourish.
'Blood and bone on a rubbish dump,'
he says.
'Blood and bone.
That's the secret.'

Sr. Sandra Sears CSBC

How dare the cross?

How dare the cross
be an object of worship,
a source of devotion,
a comfort to the sinful?

Not beautiful but gruesome –
suffering is not glorious:
it's a testament to folly
and human depravity.

The wonder is that you forgave
those who persecuted you,
that your love shone through
the darkness of humanity.

In you we see fulfilment,
the best humanity can be.
You did not die in my place –
you showed me the Way.

Judith Jessop

Good Friday in any town

Our churches gather in his name
to walk behind the Cross of shame.

The soldiers swill and yell for more –
they've done this many times before –
nailed some poor bastard to a cross.
They've had their fun, he'll be no loss;
there's girls to bed and dice to toss.
'I thirst,' he says. There's one to hear
and offer wine on sponge-tipped spear.

A man enjoys a hot-cross bun
while hanging there is Mary's son.
Blood soaks the ground. His words are few
but looking down, he thinks of you,
the son you bore but hardly knew,
'Dear faithful friend, your mother, John,
and you her son when I have gone.'

The town perceives no holy day
though Christians on the pavement pray,
though now an earthquake splits the rocks
and the Temple shakes in aftershocks.
But sport is showing on the box.
While balls are kicked and horses run
how few mourn God's forsaken son.

Come, friend, and see where he is laid –
while Tesco does a roaring trade.

Iris Lloyd

Postmodern

God
what does a postmodern Christian
think and pray about on Good Friday?

The theology I was taught in my childhood and adolescence,
Jesus dying for my sins,
an angry Father,
an obedient Son,
redeeming blood,
a sacrificial lamb,
it doesn't make sense any more,
if it ever really did.

I think of you now as all-loving.
I don't have a problem that I can no longer think of you as almighty,
all-loving is more than enough.

The life and stories of Jesus still grab me.
All that wisdom and courage and justice,
the call to love you with everything I am,
to practise kindness and justice with all of my neighbours,
to respect and love and get to know myself.

You still call me.
I'm still Christian.
Hearing you in Jesus,
seeing you in creation,
meeting you in my neighbours,
knowing deep inside that I am loved and valued and taken seriously:
God – I love you for all that.

And I pray,
I still pray.
I think the way that you intervene in this world is through the hands and minds and hugs and tears of people who try to be kind and just and loving,
so I pray ...
for people I know,

for people whose stories are in the news,
for those in authority,
for those who are sad, or in pain or trouble,
for those who are happy,
for those living in hard places,
for those being born,
for those who are dying,
for those who are full of life.

And I ask you to keep me loving,
to remind me that honesty, forgiveness, reconciliation and wonder
are still on your agenda,
and to lead me, with a smile, into wisdom and truth.

Loving God,
hear my thoughts and prayers this Good Friday.
I bring them thoughtfully and joyfully to you.

Ruth Burgess

The good guy

Good Friday.

What is good about it?

What could be good about remembering the day Jesus died?

It is a sad story that shows how horrible people can be. A story about the nasty, terrible things that were done to Jesus on the day he died. There were soldiers hitting him and spitting on him. There were people making fun of him and calling him names. There were people shouting out that if he was really someone special – why couldn't he get himself out of trouble?

And where were all Jesus' friends when he was being hit and spat on and shouted at and made fun of? Most of them had run away, scared that they might get into trouble too. Only his mum and some other women stuck by him, but they knew they could not stop the soldiers from hurting Jesus. And they did not want to get hurt themselves, so they kept quiet. They just followed in the crowd as Jesus was pushed and shoved along the road outside the big city of Jerusalem. He was taken to a place called Golgotha, and that was where he died. Poor Jesus.

Is there anything good about this story at all?

What do you think Jesus did when the soldiers hit him?

What might he have been thinking as they spat on him?

Have you ever been called names or had someone laugh at you?

What did you want to do?

What do you think Jesus did?

Jesus did not hit back or spit back. Neither did he say anything bad to the people who were laughing and jeering at him. He was bullied and pushed around and called names. But he wouldn't let anyone make him behave the same way. No matter how horrible anyone was to Jesus on that sad day, he did nothing horrible back to them. Jesus kept on being the good guy, right to the end!

How brave was that! One good thing in a very sad story.

Jo Love, Spill the Beans

Judas

I read that
Judas later changed his mind.
He returned all 30 of those pieces of silver.

They buried the money.
As if the crime could be hidden.

I wonder who found it.
Did someone return by cloak of darkness?
Did someone scrape away the soil in desperation?
Did a small child find shiny treasures many years later?

And, I wonder,
what do I bury deep inside,
instead of trusting

the healing light of forgiveness?

Fiona van Wissen

Pietà

Mother of sorrows, cradling my dead son.
Such an ignominious death. Shocking
to think of it. His face startled everyone.
Seems like yesterday he started walking
those first steps leading him away from me.
I never understood him much. Such passion
he had for change. Could never let things be.
Upsetting people, challenging the fashion
for the Roman way. Talked much of God's love.
It is finished now. No marks except this
long red cut. My fingers trace his face above
remembering with pain his childhood kiss.

Your former friends have gone. My grief they shun.
Why have they forsaken us, Judas, my son?

Mary Hanrahan

Nicodemus

Why am I doing this?
Why have I chosen now, of all times, to come out into the open?
He's dead, his real friends have deserted him
and who is left?
Me, Joseph and a few women.
Not much of a following after three years' hard work.
What good am I doing?
When he was alive I went to see him secretly, by night.
His answers to my questions weren't exactly comforting.
Now he's dead, why am I here?
Creeping towards his tomb,
laden like a donkey,
hoping none of the Sanhedrin will see me.
And what my wife will say
when she learns I've bought thirty-four kilos of spices
I can't imagine.
No, that's a lie –
I can imagine it very well.

Why am I here?
I honestly don't know.
In life he helped many people;
all he did for me was make my head spin.
But now he's in need
and none of his real supporters seem to be around.
So it's left to me.
I can make sure that he has a decent burial,
that at least I can do.

Brian Ford

Holy Saturday

Come Saturday

Come Saturday

Mary, MM and Sally
were rearranging
the furniture
and cleaning up
the mess
from Friday's wake;

the guys,
who'd found their loss
uneased
no matter how much
they consumed last night,
took double doses
of painkillers
and stumbled back
to bed;

Jesus
lay in the chill
of the darkness,
his head cradled
in God's lap,
while she stroked
his hair,
humming the
Resurrection Lullaby;

come Saturday …

Thom M Shuman

A service in a graveyard

Today is Easter Saturday.
Yesterday we remembered the death of Jesus.
Tomorrow we will celebrate his resurrection.
But today is Easter Saturday – it is not time for Easter eggs yet.

Today is a day we are encouraged to think about life and death.
To wonder what happens to us when we die.
Today we are encouraged to be still, to let God hold us in the silence.

Traditionally Easter Saturday is the day that Jesus descended into Hell
and set free the captives.
In death as in life Jesus tells the story of God's redeeming love.

Whatever we make of this tradition there is truth behind it.
Jesus is no stranger to death. He has been there before us.
Death and life are part of who we are and always will be.

On Easter Saturday we remember those who have died
and know them to be safe in God.

Listen to some words from the Bible:

Luke 4:16–19

Romans 8:38–39

A hymn or a chant (see Notes)

Suggested action:

After we have closed this service with a blessing you are invited to come and take a daffodil – and to lay it on a grave in this graveyard. You may choose to lay it on a familiar grave or on the grave of a stranger. You are invited to read the words on the stone, if there is one, and to remember the person who lies there and pray for their friends and family.

You may want to think about those who are dying, or who will die today.

You may want to remember friends and family who are buried or have their ashes scattered elsewhere.

Give yourself time and permission to grieve: for someone you love, for lost opportunities, for unfulfilled dreams ...

Take your time in the graveyard.

It is a good place to be between the crucifixion and the resurrection.

Blessing:

The blessing of God the Maker be upon us –
a blessing of beauty and wonder.
The blessing of Jesus be among us –
a blessing of trust and courage.
The blessing of the Holy Spirit be in us –
a blessing of love and life.
Amen

Notes:

Using chants means that you can lead this service without a service paper. Suggestions: 'Jesus, remember me', CH4 775; 'Ipharadisi', Freedom Is Coming, *Wild Goose Publications; 'Wonder and stare',* Come All You People, *John L. Bell, Wild Goose Publications. Suggested songs: 'When we are living', CH4 726, 'Give thanks for life', CH4 736*

You need twice as many cut daffodils for this service as you expect participants (some people will take more than one).

You may chose readings from other sources as well as from the Bible. Stanbrook Abbey has an office hymn for Easter Saturday, 'His Cross stands empty in a world grown silent'.

Ruth Burgess

Why is it holy?

Holy Saturday.

Why is it holy, this Second Day?
Most of us don't think so, or ignore it,
or subsume it under Easter,
as 'Easter Saturday';

but Easter hasn't happened yet.

The bereaved need time
in which there are no tears or smiles:
only a huge blankness
numbness
shock.

Our world lives in the Second Day.
It thinks that everything it once believed in
is dead,
while daily life goes demandingly, coldly on.

We have locked ourselves up
in grief and disenchantment and despair,
rocking quietly in the dark,
or sealed ourselves behind unyielding 'strength'
designed to keep the truth at bay.

Wisdom bids us rest,
allow the tears,
sleep,
eat what we can.

We need today because
we are worn out.
Tomorrow is unimaginable
but it will come.
Not an embalming of what's gone for good,
but something startling,

unrecognisable,
new.

Tomorrow, some of us will get up early to go and look,
and most of us will not.
The news will get out, just the same,
and today is still holy, though we are unaware.

Sue Sabbagh

An aching place

There is a place,
an aching place.
A nowhere,
neither-here-nor-there place;
longing, liminal,
where all the pain of the world is gathered up.
Its floor is engraved
with the prayers
of those who have dared
to wait there.
Who have reached out
to touch the tears of God.

Sr. Sandra Sears CSBC

Piercings

Teacher, inspector, a restless class.
I had been advised. '*Go easy on him.*
They're a difficult lot to manage
and she's quite capable of wrecking his plans altogether.
Loud. Can't wait to get out. He's doing his best
to pull them through the syllabus before the exam.
You'll spot her straightaway. And the rest.'

So I have sympathy as he struggles
to take them through the story of an ancient passion,
sufferings and betrayal new as today,
stumbling at horror,
wondering at a daybreak, two days after.

'So where' (he was sweating) *'d'you think
he went. What was he doing, those hours
after death and burial?'*

The silence lasts for aeons.

His eyes flicker hopefully to the front,
the predictable tryers.
The class stirs and shuffles, sighs.
Shrugs its corporate body.

Girl with piercings
of lips and brow,
black-nailed tips to fingers, hair spiked into thorns.
Jumper ragged over wrists to hide the slashes.
Her hand raised. *'Sir.
Sir.'*
I see his eyes shift. The door, the window,
the front row. Nothing.
'Sir.'

'Yes, Della?' (O God, no, he begs.)
'That's easy, innit,' she says.
*'He went to Hell to find his friend Judas.
He'd lost his friend. He went to find him.'*

An indrawn breath.
Theology rocks.

Girl, Goth. Moth at the candle of self-harm,
just so He will find you, even in its flame.

Janet Killeen

Holy Saturday is longer than a day

Holy Saturday

… is longer than a day.
For it takes time
to delve into the depths,
to feel weightily
pain and loss and letting go.

It takes time
to shout and grieve,
to honour deep within
the changed reality.

It takes time
to signify meaning,
to sense discomfort,
cathartic tears in flow.

It takes time
to understand God's love,
to be aware of His presence,
knowing you are upheld.

It takes time
to be prepared,
to embrace possibilities,
to believe in hope.

Holy Saturday

… is longer than a day.

Judith Jessop

Easter Vigil

Get ready

It is possible
to so live in the dark
to creep into despondency
to wallow in hurt and anger

that you miss
the emerging glow of life
the promise near fruition
the renewal of hopefulness.

Look carefully at your feet:
see the grounded growth.
Lift expectantly your eyes:
look to the horizon.

See, feel, hear
the faint clamour
of resurrection.

Get ready
to leave your refuge.

Judith Jessop

Dying to life

Perhaps the old form of faith
must die, fall into the dust
and return to its beginning,
that new life, freed and unfettered,
may rise.

Perhaps the tomb is naught to fear,
the darkness an unravelling,
a comfort and a rest.

Perhaps light comes stealthily,
and garments become threadbare,
and radiance grows from within.

Perhaps the great letting go is a letting be,
an acceptance and a grace,
that life may spring up,
radiance meeting radiance,
wonder comprehending wonder.

Carla Grosch-Miller

You have brought us from darkness into light (an Easter Vigil prayer of thanksgiving)

Creator God, you have brought us from darkness into light.
Alleluia!

Word of God, Christ, you have brought us through the waters,
from death into life.
Alleluia!

Life-giving Spirit of God, you move among us,
making of us a new creation.
Alleluia!

In your dying, you have destroyed our death.
All that required us to be who we were,
all that separated us from you, is gone.
Help us to continue to turn from sin, every day,
to work every day to remove the conditions of death,
the causes of death,
and the attitudes of death,
from the world around us.

In your rising, you have restored our life.
Where, before, we had only a fate, now we have possibilities.

Lead us to foster life wherever we are,
through our actions,
through our relationships,
through our economics.

In your living among us, you have transformed our life.
No longer does our survival need to be our chief focus, our chief end.
Challenge us to live for others,
and, in living for others, to live for you,
and to have you live eternally in us.

By your will and because of your boundless love for us
we find ourselves standing on the threshold
between old creation and new,
looking at a world filled with your life and love.
By your grace, walk with us into Easter and beyond;
help us see where, even amid the shadows of the old life,
your new life awaits us;
help us, every day, to embrace hope rather than fear,
joy rather than anger,
life rather than death,
all in the name of Christ,
who died on our behalf and rose to show us the way,
and who taught us to pray with joy, saying …

Our Father …

James Hart Brumm

The light keeps getting brighter now

The light keeps getting brighter now.
Alleluia!

Christ's light is making everything clear.
Alleluia!

Once we knew what the world was:
limited, painful, familiar.
Now Christ has opened up your new creation,
and we are excited and a bit afraid.
Alleluia!

This morning, among the dead,
as on that first morning among the dead,
the promise of eternity with you
has become real.
Alleluia!

We came here, one by one.
We leave as the risen body of Christ.
Help us to let go of what has past
and to embrace all the world in your name.
Help us to joyfully shout:
'The Lord is risen indeed!'

Easter has begun again!
Let every day be Easter in our hearts.
Alleluia! Amen!

James Hart Brumm

Easter Morning

Darkness before dawn

Waking in the darkness before dawn,
I step out.
Birdsong greets my ears:
I pause, listen,
drink in the morning chorus.

Yet,
the silent song of my heart
perches precariously on a dry branch.

Waiting for spring.
Waiting for freedom.
Waiting for resurrection.

Fiona van Wissen

Birds still sing

The sun has still risen,
birds still sing,
people are getting up, having breakfast, setting out for work,
as if nothing has happened.
As if it's just the beginning of another ordinary week.
I want to climb a hill,
stand on a wall,
clamber up onto a roof
and shout:
'He's dead!
The best man who ever lived –
and more than that.
The one man who didn't deserve to be punished –
and you killed him!
The greatest injustice ever.

And I abandoned him,
ran away,
and then denied I knew him.'

Some of the women have gone to the tomb,
to finish work on the body.
Why?
I can see them in the distance,
returning,
rushing back,
running, looking flustered.
Why?
There can be absolutely nothing to get excited about now,
can there?

Brian Ford

A gathering prayer

God of resurrection,
you have rolled the stone away
and the tomb of our world
has been opened wide.
With the dawn has come a new creation.
Let our celebration today
empty our tombs,
renew our lives
and release your power;
through the risen Christ we pray.
Amen

James Hart Brumm

The angel

'And suddenly there was a great earthquake, for an angel of the Lord, descending from heaven, came and rolled back the stone and sat on it.' (Mt 28:2, NRSV)

Sorry, did I hear that right?

'For an angel of the Lord ... rolled back the stone and *sat* on it'!

Have you ever wondered about that?

It seems so commonplace,
sitting on a stone.
It sets me wondering
how the angel was sitting.
From the reactions of those
reported to be there, we can tell
that he was probably a bit overwhelming –
after all, it is not every day
one sees an angel of the Lord!
But was he sitting with authority,
looking stern
(albeit with a twinkle in his eye!),
in such a way it frightened the guards
so they 'became like dead men'?

I can't help thinking,
after everyone had gone,
did he perhaps relax a bit and sit
chuckling, legs swinging gleefully?

But no,
I'm sure that's not what happened either ...

The God of all,
Creator and Saviour of the World,
had just overcome death
to bring humanity back to God.

No, that angel didn't sit on the stone –
he danced on it!

Mel Perkins

Spinning the story

A dialogue between an unnamed scribe and the gospel writer John on how best to record the events around the Resurrection. It should be read with a bit of fun and irony.

Scribe: How are we going to write the next bit of the story?

John: Well, we've given Joseph and Nicodemus a high profile for the burial, so that should keep a balance.

Scribe: Good thinking. We won't mention names for the Sunday morning tomb scene.

John: I don't think we can get away without naming Mary. Maybe the others we can gloss over.

Scribe: We can say that she went straight to the men anyway. It makes her look a bit clueless.

John: Brilliant! But did she? Can we be sure about that?

Scribe: We can sound sure. Who's going to argue? Our proofreaders are men!

John: Ha ha, indeed! So how do we keep the focus where we want it for the next part?

Scribe: Well, Peter should be named, and maybe another, yourself even?

John: Modesty forbids! I could self-refer, of course, in a disguised manner … how about 'the one whom Jesus loved'?

Scribe: Subtle.

John: And I thought we could have a few words about us seeing the grave clothes before she did, and, you know, piecing it all together, so to speak …

Scribe: Even though it's actually taken us years … and we probably still haven't got it …

John: Get a grip! You're sounding like a woman!

Scribe: How can we possibly tell the next bit without giving Mary her place?

John: I know, I know. Well, we've got her in tears for a start. Full of uncertainty. Not knowing who Jesus is. And trying to cling on to him.

Scribe: But still, he chose her to be the first. A woman. The first to see him, to touch him, to proclaim he was alive. He chose her over one of us!

John: There are some things we can't get away from, it's true. I'm working on bringing things back round to people like Thomas, and adding a lot more about Peter, so that we can finish up with the right emphasis.

Scribe: And I suppose we've managed to tone down the women's involvement while Jesus was on the road and teaching.

John: Exactly. I've made a few concessions of course: his mother at the wedding, the Samaritan at the well, and the adulteress escaping a good stoning. I had to name Martha and Mary: fair's fair, they do seem to have been quite important to him. You can understand that though, with one being a great cook and the other a dab hand at massage. A man needs to be fed and pampered.

Scribe: Do you really think that's all he saw in them?

John: They're women! What else would he see?

Scribe: Well … let me think … debating skills, good listening, hospitality, theological understanding, devotion, reliability, financial generosity, trust, perseverance, strength of spirit, powers of perception, friendship, compassion, intelligence, courage, integrity, loyalty, negotiating skills, wit, wisdom, intimacy, solidarity, the fine balance of honesty and diplomacy …

John: Surely Jesus can't expect us to spell that out! Can you imagine where it would lead?

Scribe: He asked us to follow.

John: We're giving quite enough clues where he stood with women. We're writing a story here, not trying to turn the world upside down.

Scribe: He said 'the last will be first. And the lowly will be lifted up'. Maybe he meant it … I'm just saying.

John: She was the first, and I'll let that stand. We can only hope nobody thinks it through.

Jo Love, Spill the Beans

Easter according to John's Gospel

Use some or all of the voices

Mary:

It was still dark when I got there.
He was dead – I knew that –
but I still wanted to be near him.

It had been a horrible death
hard – so hard – to watch
but we were there for him:
his mother, his aunt, me and another Mary
and John, the disciple that he loved.

We had heard him say it,
'It is finished'
and then he was dead.

Finished – ended – over
and still dark.

As the sun rose I saw that
the stone was no longer in front of his tomb.

And I ran.

I ran to find Mary, his mother,
who was staying with John,
and Peter was there too.

And I told them
that his body
wasn't there.

Peter:

She told us
out of breath from running
she told us
and we had to see for ourselves.

John ran faster than me
he was fitter – younger –
and he got there first
and he stood outside the tomb
looking – but not going in.

I caught up
and I pushed past him
we were both breathless

The linen wrappings that Nicodemus
and Joseph had so tenderly wrapped around his body
lay on the floor
and the cloth they had tied around his head was there too
rolled up, all by itself.

John came in and stood beside me
he looked stunned
the way he looked sometimes
when Jesus was explaining something to him.

What could we do?
Neither of us knew what was happening.

We came out of the cave
and we went home.

An angel:

We were standing in the tomb
where they had laid him
the air was electric.

We had been sent there to meet Mary
and ask her a question
but she was still outside the tomb crying
but we knew she would look in again soon and see us
and she did.

And we asked her,
'Woman, why are you crying?'
And she told us:
'They have taken the body of Jesus, my rabbi, away,
and I don't know where they've put him.'

We knew what had happened
but we couldn't tell her.

And, still crying, she went out into the garden.

Mary:

I'd come back.

I knew John and Peter were way ahead of me
and by the time I reached the garden
they'd gone.

I was alone.

I thought I'd have no tears left
but I was still weeping …

When I looked again into the tomb I could see two angels
and they asked me why I was still crying.

They were angels – God's messengers – surely they knew why I was crying!

I walked away from the tomb and I heard someone ask me a question.
It was a man – he had his back to me –
and he asked me who I was looking for.
I assumed he was the gardener
and I asked him if he had moved Jesus' body
and he turned round
and he said my name
'Mary'
and I knew.

I knew he was alive.

It wasn't the gardener – it was Jesus!

I wanted to hug him for ever and ever – to feel his strength, his love,
his kindness – to never let him go.

But he told me to go and find Peter and John and tell them
what had happened
and I did.

But I told Mary what had happened first
for she was his mother.

Jesus:

It's strange
this body
it feels like it's always done
but it's different.

I wanted to hug her
but I wasn't sure if I could
wasn't sure if she could hug me back.

But I could speak to her.
I could tell her how much I loved her
for her tears, her care, her wonder.

In the end I just said her name
and it was enough.

She recognised who I was
and she knew.

She knew that
our worlds had been turned upside down.

And we both recognised our own hesitancy
our own shyness
and our deep love for each other.
I think it may take
the disciples longer
to grasp what has happened.

But Mary knew
and she'll be my witness.

And one day
very soon
my disciples will know too.

Narrator:

Mary wondered
and Mary met him
and Mary knew
and Mary whispered,
'Jesus is alive.'

The angels knew
for God had told them
and the angels whispered,
'Jesus is alive.'

John wondered
and John saw the tomb was empty
and John knew
and John whispered,
'Jesus is alive.'

We wonder
and we ask questions
and we can meet him
and we can whisper,
'Jesus is alive.'

It's Easter morning.
Forget the whispering.
Feel like shouting?
OK – let's do it.
On the count of three
take a deep breath …
one, two, three –
'Jesus is alive.'

Ruth Burgess

Mad Mary

'But the apostles thought that what the women said was nonsense.' Luke 24:11

Mad Mary, they called me. Well, I was pretty mad in those days. People were frightened of me – sometimes I was frightened of myself. I saw and heard things that weren't there; quite often I had visions of my dead mother or of angels, and I quickly acquired a reputation in Magdala and the surrounding area. Some people thought I was a witch; the priests tried to cure me a few times, but it never helped, and I got worse. My father died and I was left alone with my insanity. I felt like a collection of broken fragments that I had no idea how to put together – I craved companionship but my wild talk scared people away. People told their children not to come near me – that really hurt; I would never have harmed anyone and I would have loved a husband and children of my own, but such relationships as I had with men were brief and sometimes violent. Decent men would have nothing to do with me; the other kind were happy to take advantage of me when the loneliness drove me into their arms, but there was never any chance of peace and happiness with the kind of people I chose.

I hated myself for my behaviour, but I didn't know how to be any other way. Once or twice the pain was so great that I tried to kill myself – not succeeding, I cursed God for letting me live on in such agony. What was the point of a life such as mine? I was no use to anyone and a burden to myself. After the last unsuccessful suicide attempt I remember getting very drunk and standing outside the Temple screaming at God: 'Either help me or let me die!' I was lucky not to be arrested that day – fortunately an old neighbour of my parents was passing and saw the state I was in. She took me home and calmed me down; she'd known me from a child and wasn't scared of me, but it distressed her to see me so unhappy.

'There's a new healer travelling around the area,' she said, 'maybe he could help you. He's helped a lot of people – remember Tobias' boy with the fits? He's not had a single seizure since this Jesus laid hands on him. Really, Mary, he's different from the priests. I've seen him and heard him speak. Shall I take you to see him?'

I was too miserable to take in what she was saying so I agreed, with no idea how dramatically my life was to change. Well, you know the rest – how I met

Jesus and joined his company, and what happened to him, and what happened after that. It's still a source of wonder to me that I was so special to him. Of course after our meeting I fell violently in love with him, but rather than being embarrassed or uncomfortable about it, he seemed to accept it. He let me stay close to him, held me when I got upset, but never took advantage of me; and his calm affection gradually settled the storms in my mind and I discovered a sense of security and peace I'd never known before. Peter and the rest didn't like me at first and couldn't understand why Jesus let me go with them. I overheard Peter arguing with him once about it:

'Jesus, the woman's crazy – she's an embarrassment. Everyone thinks you're having an affair with her. What kind of Messiah are you going to be if you let someone with her reputation follow you around?'

But Jesus just smiled and let him rant on until he ran out of steam, then said, 'She needs to be with us, Peter, and we need her. She has tremendous gifts.' Peter nearly exploded at that. I was amazed. 'Gifts'! What gifts did I have?

It was true though. As my mind began to settle I discovered that my uncanny sensitivity and ability to hear and see things wasn't just a product of my insanity – I really did have some kind of sixth sense. Jesus took me with him on some of his healing work, and I found that sometimes I knew what was wrong with people before they told us. I began to acquire the courage and confidence to pray and lay hands on the sick myself, and to my amazement sometimes they got well. After a few spectacular healings in which I was involved, people stopped laughing and nudging each other when they saw us coming and began to treat me with something I'd never experienced – respect. Even better, I started to respect myself. I saw myself as Jesus saw me: not a crazy, out of control woman, but as somebody lovable and likeable with God-given gifts.

I thought I was close to him, but I still wasn't prepared for the terrible events of that Passover. He had tried to explain, but none of us understood. Right up until the last moment I think I still believed that it wasn't really going to happen; somehow he wouldn't die. The earthquake and thunder on the hill that day were nothing compared to the turmoil in my mind as I stood there paralysed, watching the life ebb away from him. We were all completely numb with horror and disbelief. For a time I thought I would return to that uncontrolled insanity – Jesus had been all that was holding me together, and with him dead I feared my mind was going to disintegrate. But somehow the strength I had gained during our time together came to my rescue.

The men just panicked; overcome with terror of meeting the same fate, they scattered in all directions, but we women stuck together and managed to calm ourselves with the practical tasks of collecting the spices and balms we needed for anointing the body. I was determined that we would at least do that for him; I had loved his body as I had loved the rest of him, and I wasn't going to see it just slung into a hole in the ground with no preparation.

We were taking a risk of course – we knew that the tomb was guarded and we might be arrested. Some of the women changed their minds and backed down; we had the whole of the Sabbath to worry about it and in the end only three of us went. On the way I suddenly remembered that the tomb had been closed, and was devastated with disappointment – there was no way we would be able to move the stone ourselves. However, we decided to go anyway – even if we couldn't embalm Jesus' body we could at least say some prayers and pay our respects.

Nothing could have prepared me for the shock of finding the tomb open and the body gone. I had been holding myself together mentally by a great effort – I knew in my mind that he was dead, but needed to see and touch his corpse to make it real, and comfort myself by doing this last service for him. I had never dared tell him how much I loved him when he was alive – patient as he was, there always still lurked in me the fear that he would reject me if he knew how I really felt. But now I couldn't even do that.

The other women tried to pull me away, terrified that the grave-robbers might come back and kill us, but I couldn't have cared less. I searched the tomb, felt the walls, dug at the floor with my nails, clutched the discarded wrappings in my arms and hugged them to my chest as if I could hold on to my dead friend forever. I couldn't bear the thought of his body being violated, left naked on some hillside to rot. Nor could I understand why anyone would want to steal it; there was nothing to steal – unless the brigands knew the tomb belonged to Joseph of Arimathea and assumed that any friend of his must have been buried with gold and jewels beside him.

Eventually Mary and Joanna gave up and left me to my misery. The sun was up and it was getting hot; they had families to care for and things to do. I remained in the dim coolness of the tomb, sunk in agony. Where could I go now, what would I do? My life had lost all its meaning, and despair picked at the edges of my sanity. I knew that Judas had committed suicide, and I could understand why; it was a long time since such thoughts had troubled me, but the old blackness was closing in on me and I had no defence against it. Jesus had been my defence, but he had abandoned me and I was alone.

I lay on the damp floor of the tomb, shivering with shock and fear, inhaling the musty smell of the earth, still holding my little bag of spices. Suddenly I became aware that a beam of sunlight had shone through the entrance and was warming my back. I looked up – the whole tomb was full of a blinding light and I scrambled to my feet – dazzled. Some overwhelming force threw me to the wall and I flattened myself against it; I could hear a roar of joy and adulation inside my head, like the day we came into Jerusalem – only a million times louder. It was as if every creature on earth was singing and cheering and making as much noise as it could. I thought my head was going to burst, and in the middle of it all I could hear a shouting: 'He's alive! He's alive! He's not here!' I realised that I was shouting and cheering and dancing in the light; my ears were filled with the sound of song and music and I sang along with it in an unknown language – then suddenly the light faded, the sounds stopped, and I was alone again in the empty tomb. But not alone: I knew with utter certainty that Jesus was alive; I would see him again. I tore open the bag of spices and scattered them round the floor; the perfume filled the tomb as I sank to the ground in tears of joy and gratitude. Then I came to my senses. I had to tell the others – they would be overjoyed. I sprang to my feet and raced out into the sunlight, back to Jerusalem – people gazed at me in amazement as I ran past but I was too excited to care what I looked like. I panted up to the house where I knew the others were hiding, and hammered on the door.

Peter and Andrew leapt to their feet in panic as I charged into the room, then relaxed when they realised it was me.

'Peter! James! He's gone!' I cried. 'The tomb's empty! He's alive! I've seen him. Oh, it's wonderful – I'm so happy ...'

Peter and Andrew looked at each other. I chattered on, laughing and crying at the same time, running from one to the other, impatient to make them listen.

'Come on, come to the tomb – you have to see, I'll show you …'

None of them moved. I pulled at Peter's arm, trying to drag him towards the door, but he shook me off and started leading me to a chair.

'Now, Mary,' he said kindly, 'you're overwrought. This has been a very upsetting time for us all and I'm sure it must have affected you. I know you were very fond of Jesus, but you have to accept that he's gone. Sit here and let me get you a glass of wine.'

'Leave me alone, you idiot,' I snapped. 'Don't you understand what I'm telling you? He said this would happen, he told us …'

But it was no use. The expression on Peter's face said it all. To him I would always be a crazy unstable woman whose word carried no more weight than a child's, and the others took their cue from him. Tears of frustration sprang to my eyes as he patted my shoulder soothingly and pressed a cup into my hand. He fussed about like an old mother hen; a plate of food appeared in front of me and I realised how hungry I was. My anger began to dissipate – I knew what I had experienced and my joy was complete. Perhaps I just had to be patient. Peter had always been a bit slow to cotton on to what Jesus was getting at, and he hadn't seen what I had seen, so why should he believe me?

'If it makes you happy, Mary,' he was saying, 'I'll go and have a look myself. There now – will that help?'

I had to work very hard not to laugh when he came back all crestfallen. He wouldn't say exactly what he had seen but mumbled something about funny tricks of the light. But soon it didn't matter – Jesus made himself known to all of us. I saw him more than once – somehow he knew that my insecurity needed his attention, and provided the certainty that I required to be an effective witness. I couldn't believe that he had chosen me – the least credible, the least confident – to be the first to see him, the first to know the good news. But he had – and people flocked to me, eager to hear the story over and over again. I never tire of telling it – not just what happened in the tomb, but my own story and what happened to me. To my mind that's almost more miraculous – how mad Mary became a seer, a prophet, a witness to the truth, when once my word had been as worthless as a bunch of straw.

Catherine Harkin

Conversation with a gardener

No, Mary Magdalene wasn't asking for the gardener.
No one expects you to be at work before sunrise.
Yes, that would certainly be most unreasonable.
I know you've always put in a fair day's work for a fair day's pay
and you've worked here man and boy for over fifty years.
You've told me so,
many times.

Mary actually mistook Jesus for the gardener.
No, he isn't after your job.
Yes, he is a carpenter.
No, he probably couldn't tell an aquilegia from an artichoke,
although he was interested in flowers.
Yes, I am absolutely satisfied with your work.
I wouldn't dream of replacing you.

Yes, I am sorry the guards abused your geraniums,
and picked your best pansies,
and Peter trampled all over your petunias,
and that stone crushed some of your best sweet peas when it moved.
You see, something very remarkable happened in the garden last night.
It was far, far more important
than a few vandalised flowers and wrecked plants,
believe it or not.

Brian Ford

Resurrection

It's the little things that live in memory,
that touch the heart,
that herald hope.

Blinded by tears,
heavy with grief.

In the garden
the world was re-created,
wonder born afresh,
as He softly said her name.
'Mary.'

Mary Hanrahan

An Easter prayer of confession

Almighty God,
through the rising of your son from the grave,
you broke the power of death
and condemned death itself to die.
Yet, even as you open this new way for us,
we find ourselves too often drawn to the old ways.
We too often forget to love you with all that we are.
We too rarely love neither our neighbours nor ourselves.

God of Easter glory, as we celebrate this triumph,
help us to make it the model for our living.
Help us to identify all in us that should rightly die:
redundant relationships, tired habits, fruitless longings.
Resurrect in us faith, hope and love
as surely as you have raised Jesus Christ from the grave.

James Hart Brumm

An Easter morning communion

Invitation:

On this resurrection morning, fresh from the garden,
Jesus bids us to come dine with him.

On this resurrection morning, though we are still unsure of who he is,
Jesus bids us to come dine with him.

On this resurrection morning,
though we know how easily we falter in our faith,
Jesus bids us to come dine with him.

Bible reading: *Matthew 26:26–30*

While they were eating, Jesus took bread, and when he had given thanks, he broke it and gave it to his disciples, saying, 'Take and eat; this is my body.'

Then he took a cup, and when he had given thanks, he gave it to them, saying, 'Drink from it, all of you. This is my blood of the covenant, which is poured out for many for the forgiveness of sins. I tell you, I will not drink from this fruit of the vine from now on until that day when I drink it new with you in my Father's kingdom.'

When they had sung a hymn, they went out to the Mount of Olives.

Jesus, knowing that he was about to be betrayed and handed over to the authorities, shared a meal with his disciples. Before they scattered into the approaching storm and deserted him, he gave them this memorial which would bring them back together and speak to them of forgiveness and union with God and with each other.

These symbols before us today speak of forgiveness and communion with God and with each other, and on this Easter Day, they speak to us too of the wonder of resurrection.

Prayer of thanksgiving and intercession:

Risen Lord Jesus,
that night in the upper room with your disciples,
as you looked around the table, you knew who would betray you.
You knew who would desert you.
You knew who would be too weary to watch for you.
Yet you looked at each of your friends with love.
In our weakness, in our failings, in our weariness,
still you love us.

We give thanks for this sacrament that unites us with you
and with each other,
that restores our souls and nourishes our spirit.
As we share this feast today, may we know the depth of healing,
the depth of loving and the depth of restoration that is possible
in the new life you offer.
May we know your healing and love flooding our lives with warmth
and overflowing into the communities we serve.

We remember those who live in fear,
those who live without hope,
those who live without love.

As we feel your resurrection stir our souls in this place today,
surrounded by your Spirit,
and the spirits of all those saints who have gone before us,
may we be renewed in purpose,
taking the power and the energy of your love into the world –
knowing that your love changes everything.

God, breathe your resurrection Spirit
into this bread and this wine,
that we may know your risen power
infusing all that we do and share together,
enabling us to go and breathe new life into the world.

Breaking and sharing:

Jesus, looking into the eyes
of those he knew would fail him, took bread.
He broke it and said:
'This is my body, broken for you. Do this to remember me.'
He took the cup, already tainted by betrayal,
and spoke of forgiveness
and the new kingdom, and said:
'Drink from it all of you.'

In this bread and wine our risen Lord offers us new life today.
We do this to remember him.
See the risen Lord striding toward you today,
holding out life in all its fullness.

Share bread and wine.

Prayer after Communion:

Lord Jesus, we have feasted on the bread of life.
We have quenched our thirst with the wine of your new kingdom.
In your risen power
you have united us with all our loved ones in heaven and on earth.
May that sense of communion strengthen and renew us,
bring us hope and joy,
today and in the days to come.
To you, Father, Son and Holy Spirit, one God,
be glory here and everywhere, now and forever.
Amen

Sending:

As we have worshipped, so we take our worship into the world.
When we walk uncertain into the garden – we leave rejoicing!
Where we meet the stranger – we encounter love!
When we are sent to share the news – we shout it loud!

God of yesterday, today and tomorrow,
Son of resurrection and hope,
Spirit of rejoicing hearts,
bless us,
this day and always.
Amen

Liz Crumlish, Spill the Beans

Responses before the Gospel reading

Jesus is alive and out and about –
so is God's Word alive for us!

A tomb couldn't hold the Saviour.
Printed pages can't hold God's truth!

O God, as you opened the tomb for us to see,
open our hearts for us to grow.
Amen!

James Hart Brumm

We do not claim to understand

Holy God, we are reminded of that first Easter morning
when sorrow turned to joy.
Jesus is risen from the dead.

We do not claim to understand how, but we believe it to be true.
We gather here, Sunday by Sunday, celebrating resurrection,
celebrating love that overcomes death.

Like Peter, Mary and all those who follow Jesus,
we are shocked and surprised by your power over death.
Like Peter, Mary and all those who follow Jesus,
we gather together afraid, unsure and a little anxious of what to expect.

But, as Jesus did with them, he does with us,
by coming among us and saying, 'Peace be with you.'
May that peace Jesus speaks be felt here in this place,
as we try to get our heads around resurrection once more.

Like Peter, Mary and all those who follow you, Jesus,
we come as we are, simple people, flawed and imperfect
and we offer ourselves to you.
We confess that we still have doubts,
that we still deny you at times,
that we still fail to obey your commands.
We are sorry and ask for your forgiveness.

Like Peter, Mary and all those who follow you, Jesus,
fill us with your Holy Spirit
and send us out renewed and refreshed,
ready to serve you in the world today and every day.
Amen

Spill the Beans

He is with us forever

Loving God,
we thank you for sending Jesus to be our friend.
Thank you for all the wonderful things he did.
We are sad that he died on the cross;
we are happy that he came alive again.
Thank you that he is with us forever
and that we can know your help and care each day.
Amen

Simon Taylor

Thank you

Jesus, you were always special.
You turned this world's values upside down.

Not for you the 'look-after-number-one message' of our age,
but 'look after them', you said, and you did.
Not for you the 'hold on to what you have' advice we're given,
but 'give your all', you said, and you did.
Not me first, but you first;
'not my will, but your will,' you said.
Not for you a gentle, easy birth.
Not for you a gentle, easy life.
Not for you a gentle, easy death.
Your life was never easy;
your death far from it.

But through your suffering we are free,
free to live and love right here and now,
free to live your way,
free to give, to share,
free to count all who inhabit this earth with us
as friends and neighbours,
free to be your people,
and to remember that they are your people too.
Because of what you have done,
one day, round some distant corner,
we and all who believe
will spend eternity with you.

So thank you, Jesus,
thank you for coming to us,
thank you for dying for us,
thank you for rising and living again.
Thank you that in you there is always hope.
Thank you, Jesus –
just thank you!

Gill Bailey

Earth Day

God of new life

God of new life,
whose buds grow in days of darkness
to open into increasing light,
accept our thankfulness for the beauty of springtime.
Give us patience to wait for the flowering and the fruit.
Give us joy in the harvest of your generosity.
Teach us to respect and care for the earth
and for the whole creation,
that infused with hope and expectation,
we may take our place in your plan
to reconcile all things in heaven and on earth
through the example of Christ, your Word made flesh,
whose love restores and unites.

Terry Garley

A climate of change

Though mountains be moved, they'll not overwhelm:
God has the last word, and stays at the helm.
Christ's wrestle with death, the pain he endured,
creation's true course to God's goal has secured.

Chorus: *A climate of change is now in the air*
with promise and hope displacing despair:
for not for himself did Christ rise from the dead,
but that all creation find life in its head.

But is life to end as a burnt-out shell –
our children, their children come under that spell?
The future's not ours to see – yet, for our sake
Christ died and is risen: of life we partake.

Chorus

Ian M Fraser

The silent witness of the heavens

(Metre 9.8.9.8 D, suggested tune: 'St Clement')

The silent witness of the heavens
tells of the glory of the Lord.
Vast galaxies of constellations
declare his power with one accord.
The crimson hues of fiery sunsets
and dawn-flushed clouds at morning's light,
the lightning flash, the clap of thunder
speak of his majesty and might.

The tiger prowling through the jungle,
the darting flash of hummingbird,
the snake that slithers through the desert
tell of his power without a word.
The giant redwoods in the forest,
the grandeur of the mountain's height,
the myriad life-forms in the ocean
speak of his mystery and might.

But now the land is ravaged, empty,
stripped bare by years of human greed.
And where's the justice in our taking
far more than satisfies our need?
Creation groans beneath the burden
we have imposed without a thought.
God wants us to be faithful stewards,
so let us live, then, as we ought.

Creator God, whose power we worship,
teach us to know our proper place,
to recognise the claims and value
of all, not just the human race.
Oh, help us act as proper stewards,
and understand your gift's true worth;
to make the necessary changes,
that will protect our precious earth.

Janet Pybon

Each day another species lost forever

(Metre 11.10.11.10, suggested tune: 'Intercessor')

Each day another species lost forever,
with factories that belch out deadly fumes,
and fertile farmland turning into desert,
pollution in the oceans' foaming spumes.

As ice caps melt, we lose low-lying islands,
whilst elsewhere, people face increasing drought,
yet still we hear the voices of dissension –
with all the evidence, how can they doubt?

As hungry babies die and mothers mourn them
and women raped feel pain they cannot bear,
so you, O God, who gave life to this planet,
must weep and groan and shudder with despair.

Forgive us, God, our crimes against all nature:
the selfish greed that says our needs come first,
the inequality that is our trademark,
excessive wealth whilst others starve and thirst.

Teach us to face truths that are inconvenient,
and recognise the damage that we do;
to cherish every species on this planet
and so to live that we may honour you.

Janet Pybon

Spring in April

The light of day

(Tune: 'Glasgow')

The morning light speeds on its way
to shine in every place;
it seeks to gladden every heart,
bring smiles to every face.

As light steals into every space
the dark is chased away;
this light brings colour into view
and nature starts to play.

The night and day are partners of
the cycle we know well;
like birth and death, they both embrace
the mystery where we dwell.

On Friday we could hear the pain,
the cries of tragedy;
but resurrection fashions light
that bursts with energy.

As light, which always conquers dark,
comes faithfully each day,
we constantly will praise with joy
the resurrection way.

George Stuart

I look with compassion

(Tune: 'Erin go Bragh' or 'Slane')

I look with compassion at birds in the tree
that mourn on the bough where their nest used to be,
while the jackdaws and cats take the dead chicks beneath:
as I look at them, I think God looks at me.

I wish I could nestle them safe in my hand,
and soothe them with notes that small birds understand,
or turn back the clock before death took its prey,
and scream at his servants, and drive them away.

I watch, and I weep, but I know in my heart
such help would destroy what makes birds what they are:
the balance of being in which they fly free:
as I look at them, I think God looks at me.

Except for one thing: while I mourn them in vain,
God took on our flesh, and felt pain like our pain.
And unseen as the breeze that drifts leaves to and fro
His Spirit sustains me wherever I go.

Roddy Cowie

See https://audioboom.com/posts/6061887-the-balance-of-being or https://soundcloud.com/roddy-6/balance-of-being

Upside-down God

I heard a noise in the jacaranda
and just had to go and see …
and there was God swinging
with such delight, so free.

God moved around without a care,
in such a way – I couldn't dare!

Upside down
and grinning down,
'Come and play,
not just today –
for your life-long,
come join the song,
come and follow me.'

So I threw off age
and climbed the tree,
hung by my knees
and twirled around …

and saw what God could see …

Mel Perkins

Yangtze Easter

Holy Week in Yeuyang
and daily on the waterfront
Hou Yi bends his red bow
to save the world
from the many-fanged serpent
unleashed by ten suns run amok.
The heat of one sun is enough!
Nine crow-suns must fall
to Yi's white arrows

and night by night
over Dongting Lake
there is a rending Gethsemane
of lightning and thunder,
rain sweeping the stubborn mist.

Easter Day and Tomb Sweeping Day
tumble out together
as they sometimes will
into a blue still day.
We ride a G train to Guangzhou
over 1000km in three hours
of surreal hushed motion
through Yangtze farmland
saved by ancestors
whose tombs are tucked into
little, rounded, wooded hillsides.
They learned from Hou Yi and the nine suns:

Don't Burn The Trees On The Hills!

Easter Day and Tomb Sweeping Day.
The Lord is risen! He is risen indeed!

Every tomb has been swept. Burn the litter.
The smoke is rising. It is rising indeed.

One tomb is empty. Light a fire!

Robin List

This year's diary

The winter wasn't harsh
but early March was cold and wet,
discouraging for seeking signs of spring.
Snowdrops had graced the February days
without the snow.
But signs are always there,
hazel catkins, willow flowers –
a young deer darts across the shoots of rape.
Suddenly the first green leaves appear
on hedgerows bare.
Sycamores are budding early,
wood anemones and shamrock shy on woodland floor,
open banks where primroses are clustered here and there.
Now in April we're in full spring –
morning sunshine greets the skipping lambs.
By Easter our garden thinks it's May,
glorious tulips in multicolours blaze.
Unlike the bumblebees and weeds
we can't keep up
but bask in all this lush, refreshing joy.

Liz Gregory-Smith

Thank you, God, for spring

For birds making their nests,
for eggs and chicks:
Thank you, God, for spring.

For young rabbits hopping in the fields,
for tadpoles swimming in the pond:
Thank you, God, for spring.

For bright spring flowers in the garden,
for fresh green leaves on the tree:
Thank you, God, for spring.

For longer days to play outside,
for warm sunshine on our face:
Thank you, God, for spring.

For warm hot-cross buns
and chocolate Easter eggs:
Thank you, God, for spring.

For Jesus dying to show love upon a cross,
coming alive again on Easter Day
and bringing new life to the world:
Thank you, God, for spring.
Amen

Simon Taylor

If we wait

If we wait –
keeping vigil over the bones of our dreams,
parched from too many tears.
If we wait,
there'll be a change,
a crackle,

a deep, distant boom;
a shift,
a drift of wind
that grows,
to roil around the tomb,
sweeping it clean.
Then rain –
blessed, sweet rain
dancing across our dryness,
drenching,
seeping deep down
to sleeping seeds,
laughing,
loving them into life,
growth,
greening.
If we wait,
the full will be emptied,
and the empty filled –
if we wait long enough.

Sr. Sandra Sears CSBC

Resurrection and love

There are no signposts in the desert.
Familiar ways break, disintegrate, become obsolete.
Seeking, through a mirror darkly,
we stumble into vast unknown territory.

Deep within me there is a yearning.
A desire that silently, so silently, almost imperceptibly
resonates with a desire deep within you.

And, as who you are
touches who I am.
We eclipse in a darkness that is light.
Signposts for one another
through the desert flowering of
resurrection and love.

June McAllister

Spring swings

After the long consistency of winter
spring swings crazily
from painful sun to frosty nights;
and so do I.

At my best, I am a mirror to my world.
I reflect it honestly:
and it is wild with contrary intensities;
and so am I.

Perhaps the wrecking ball that swings
from high to low to high
is clearing obsolete ruins from its ground;
and so should I.

Too easy. Winter will come again:
people will need somewhere to hide

when thunderclouds obliterate the moon's last light;
and so will I.

Spring's instant highs and lows
bed within longer cycles that swing slowly.
Things that survive adapt to both:
and so must I.

Roddy Cowie

Burgeoning

Earth stirred in his sleep,
dreams of nothingness fading phantoms.
The first shafts of April sun awoke him.
He yawned
and thousands of hibernating creatures
felt the tremor and knew it was time.
He stretched
and tired limbs of trees
felt sap rising and new buds bursting.
Earth shook the last flakes of snow
from his hair and eyelashes.
Snowdrops and bluebells sprang where they fell.
He whistled
and crowds of birds chorused his song,
harmonising, improvising, improving.
He laughed
and springs, streams and rivers tumbled
with frothing energy.
Tiny vibrations of joy filled his spirit.
Earth pulled on his green, daisy-studded waistcoat,
caught his reflection in the still lake
and whistled again.
Laughing loudly
he swaggered off
all set for his date with Spring.

Mary Hanrahan

Sacrament

Outside the hospital,
the eleven o'clock clinic over,
a small crowd gathers
to cross the road by the careful lights.

They wait for the bus to come
and scatter them home,
precarious futures carried
as a full chalice.

Grey and lined, on sticks and crutches,
waiting under the cherry trees.

And over all, drifting petal-fall spring
caresses them, touching their mortality
with gentleness.

Janet Killeen

Help us to know ourselves

As part and parcel of creation,
we breathe the air,
we share the soil
with all the creatures of the earth.

As part and parcel of God our Creator
we write, we draw,
we dance, we make music,
we listen and we do.

In times of disbelief in ourselves
remind us, God, that it is your world
and we are made in your image.

Help us to recognise your presence.
Help us to know ourselves.

Robert Shooter

The earth awakens

A liturgy for spring

Inspired by the landscape and life of Dartmoor

Opening words:

The earth awakens after winter's sleep:
Awaken us to your glory, O God.

Leaves emerge from winter's shelter and stretch out to face the sun:
Awaken us to your light, O God.

Birds that hid from frost and snow now sing out from the treetops:
Awaken us to your presence, O God.

That which seemed dead has now been born anew:
Awaken us to your life, O God.

Opening song

A song of spring (based on Song of Songs 2):

Arise, my fair ones, and come away,
for now the winter is past,
snow and frost is over and gone.

The flowers appear on the earth;
the time of singing has come.
And the song of the blackbird,
the melody of the robin
is heard in our land.

The hawthorn breaks into leaf,
the gorse opens its golden flowers,
scenting the air with fragrance.

Arise, my fair ones, and come away.
In the clefts of the rock,
in the shadow of the tor,
let us see your face.

Let us hear your voice:
for your voice is sweet
and your face is beautiful.

Prayer of confession:

O God of life,
you desire that our lives should blossom and be fruitful,
and sent your Son to die upon a cross
and be raised to life on the third day,
that new life might come to that which seemed dead.

For all that we have done that hinders life
we ask your forgiveness, Lord:

Where the striving of creation to blossom and leaf is frustrated,
where the freedom to bring new things to birth is checked,
where creativity is hindered through oppression and injustice,
where new beginnings are prevented,
where that which is needed for growth is harmed or held back,
where beauty is scarred,
where poverty and injustice allow no hope of a bright new dawn.

For all that we have done that hinders life
we ask your forgiveness, Lord:

For all that we have done to lessen the wonder of spring,
for our sin which checks the renewing of life on earth,
for negligence, carelessness and greed.

For all that we have done that hinders love
we ask your forgiveness, Lord ...

Silence

Lord, end our winter
and let your spring begin and grow in us.
Amen

Song

A spring psalm:

The sun rises higher over moorland skies;
days lengthen as night grows short:
Praise the God who gives the light.

The trees that rested through winter's cold
now awake as the earth grows warm:
Praise the God who gives the life.

Buds once tight now swell and break;
soft green leaves unfurl into the light:
Praise the God who gives the growth.

Seeds crack open and shoots emerge;
life that has been growing in secret now parts the soil:
Praise the God who brings new life to birth.

Banks of yellow primroses greet the morning sun;
blackthorn, white as frost, brightens the hedge:
Praise the God who gives the beauty.

The joyful melody of birds fills the dawn;
nests are gathered and built:
Praise the God who gives the song.

Winter gives way to spring,
just as darkness gives way to light:
So may death give way to life
as we celebrate again
the renewing of earth's green mantle.

Readings and poems

Prayers of intercession:

For all who watch and wait ...

silent or spoken prayer

God of life and new beginnings:
hear our prayers

For all who weep …

silent or spoken prayer

God of life and new beginnings:
hear our prayers

For all who long for light …

silent or spoken prayer

God of life and new beginnings:
hear our prayers

For all who are full of life …

silent or spoken prayer

God of spring,
God of death and resurrection,
God of life and new beginnings:
hear our prayers
Amen

Symbolic action:

Like planting seeds in pots for all to take away or give to others.

Closing song

Closing responses and blessing:

As the sun rises higher in the sky,
so may the Lord be exalted in our lives.

As the spring flowers display their beauty,
so may the Lord be glorified in our lives.

As the fresh green leaves on the trees announce the spring,
so may the Lord be made known in our lives.

Creator God, whose faithfulness in seen
in the coming and going of the seasons,
whose love is seen in the renewing of the earth,
guard and guide us,
keep us and bless us
now and for evermore.
Amen

Simon Taylor

An elemental blessing

A blessing of fire be yours,
of Brigid's flame
of stars and sunshine.

A blessing of water be yours,
of rain-washed streets
and huge paddling puddles.

A blessing of air be yours,
of the wild wind
and pegged washing, dancing.

A blessing of earth be yours,
of soil and roots
and green leaves unfurling.

A blessing of the elements be yours,
fire and earth and wind and water,
a blessing of hope,
a blessing of wonder,
a blessing of spring.

Ruth Burgess

About the authors

Gill Bailey: 'I am an Assembly-accredited Lay Preacher in the United Reformed Church, working in the south east area of the Wessex Synod. I'm currently studying for an MA in Theology, Imagination and Culture at Sarum College in Salisbury.

Ruth Bamforth is a teacher and music educator for all ages, and has written many songs for preschool and primary-age children, for CBeebies and for Dunblane Cathedral. She also enjoys composing Scottish country dance music and pieces for her flute and piano pupils.

Ruth Bowen lives on the island of Stronsay where she enjoys gardening and creative wool work.

James Hart Brumm is a minister of the Reformed Church in America (RCA) who teaches Theological Writing and RCA History and Worship at New Brunswick Theological Seminary. He is the author of about 300 hymns, as well as histories and articles on hymnology, liturgics and other subjects. He lives in Highland Park, New Jersey, with his wife, the Rev. Kathleen Hart Brumm.

Ruth Burgess is a member of the Iona Community living in Dunblane. She enjoys being retired and growing flowers, fruit and vegetables in her garden, which is graced by a clattering of jackdaws and a murder of crows.

Elizabeth Clark is the National Rural Officer for the Methodist and United Reformed Churches. She is passionate about rural churches and loves the countryside.

David J.M. Coleman is Environmental Chaplain for Eco-Congregation Scotland, a member of the Iona Community, a reflective digital artist and a URC minister.

Roddy Cowie is a retired professor of psychology, who did research on emotion and what is now called artificial intelligence. He has lifelong links to Iona, is a lay reader in the Church of Ireland, and is currently working on self-knowledge and Christian understanding of emotion.

Kathy Crawford has been a Reader in the Diocese of Southwell & Nottingham for 18 years and especially likes planning creative worship. In her spare time she also enjoys baking, gardening and doing word puzzles.

Tricia Creamer is a member of Poole Methodists, and runs a weekly 'Celtic Colours' group at the church, exploring Christian Spirituality through Celtic arts. She loves writing, teaching the piano, painting and is an associate member of the Iona Community.

Liz Crumlish is a Church of Scotland minister, living on the west coast of Scotland and working on Renewal. She serves on the board of RevGalBlogPals, a supportive network for women in ministry.

Judy Dinnen, priest and poet, once spent a wonderful few days on a tea plantation, high up on a Rwandan hill. She is intrigued by crosses from around the world and their stories.

Carol Dixon is a hymn writer and a lay preacher in the United Reformed Church. She and her husband live in Northumberland, are Friends of St Cuthbert's, Holy Island and enjoy days out in their caravette with their grandchildren.

Marjorie Dobson writes hymns, prayers, poetry and reflections, but her favourite challenge has always been to find a new, usually character-led, angle to a biblical story. She recently retired from her duties as a Methodist Local Preacher, but still writes material for others to use when they conduct worship.

Chris Elgood is Director Emeritus of Elgood Effective Learning, and creator of the website Praisingpiersplowman.com.

Brian Ford: 'I am a retired school teacher. My interests include gardening, poetry, folk music, Shakespeare and pantomimes.'

Sally Foster-Fulton is the Head of Christian Aid Scotland and a minister in the Church of Scotland.

Katherine Fox is a Methodist Local Preacher and civil servant living in London. She tries to help people encounter God in worship through using poetry as prayer, while also making connections to life in London.

Ian M Fraser, who died at 100 years of age in 2017, was a pastor-labourer in heavy industry, a parish minister, Warden of Scottish Churches House, an Executive Secretary of the World Council of Churches, and Dean and Head of the Department of Mission at Selly Oak Colleges, Birmingham. Throughout his life Ian travelled the world, alone and with his wife, Margaret, visiting basic Christian communities. He walked alongside slum dwellers in India and Haiti; Nicaraguan and Cuban revolutionaries; priests, nuns and catechists facing arrest and/or death in Central and South America; and small farming and fishing communities in the Philippines.

Kathy Galloway is a practical theologian and writer. She is currently one of the Co-Leaders of the Iona Community.

Terry Garley studied English, French, German and Latin before becoming a language teacher, and later a County Ecumenical Development Officer. Now gardening, reading and writing are her main pleasures in retirement.

Louise Gough is a Methodist minister in the Bramhall and Wythenshawe Circuit, Stockport. She loves playing her flute, dancing, and relaxing with her large cat, Wesley.

Liz Gregory-Smith lives in New Brancepeth, a village on the edge of Durham City. She is a retired teacher and is a Reader in the local Anglican church.

Carla Grosch-Miller is a practical theologian, educator and poet living and working from Northumberland. She is the author of *Psalms Redux: Poems and Prayers* (Canterbury Press, 2014).

Roddy Hamilton just tries to keep his head down and keep working away, yet is always amazed at what can happen and where you can find yourself when pen, paper and a little imagination come together.

Mary Hanrahan: 'Happily retired, I enjoy hobbies of crafting and writing. I am an active member of St Paul the Apostle RC church in Shettleston, and part of the Eucharistic ministry, Bereavement group and book club.'

Catherine Harkin was a member of the Iona Community, who lived and worked in Edinburgh as a GP, writer, singer and many other identities.

Pam Hathorn is a retired teacher who enjoys reading, looking at the heavens and longs to be wise.

J Mary Henderson is a Church of Scotland minister living in Falkirk and looking forward to retirement in Fife.

Judith Jessop: 'I am a Methodist pioneer minister living on a council estate in north Sheffield. I live a life of solitude in community and offer hospitality and an opportunity to explore spirituality to people struggling with church or with no connections to a faith-based community.'

Tina Kemp is associate minister at Helensburgh Parish Church linked with Rhu & Shandon. A former journalist, she has maintained her interest in writing, contributing to several church and other publications.

Janet Killeen lives in London and, since retiring from teaching, has been writing, seeking to explore questions of faith and doubt, choice and suffering that are central to her understanding of the spiritual journey. She writes poetry, has self-published two collections of short stories and her first novel, *After the Flood.*

S Anne Lawson is Vicar of the Cross Country Parishes of Acton, Church Minshull, Worleston and Wettenhall in Cheshire and Chaplain to the Cheshire Agricultural Society.

Robin List is a minister emeritus of the Presbyterian Church of Aotearoa/New Zealand. The events at the core of 'Yangtze Easter' happened while he and his wife were on a decidedly unguided birding trip during a stay in China visiting family and friends.

Iris Lloyd: 'I have been a committed Christian since the age of 17, and have been writing all my life – 20 full-length amateur pantomimes, stories, poems, plays and have recently published my eighth novel. Four years ago, I gave up dancing after eighty years. Our heavenly Father has been very generous to me and mine.'

Jo Love works with the Wild Goose Resource Group and enjoys trying to live creatively.

Rebeka Maples: 'I am Director of Spiritual Formation for a training programme of local pastors in the United Methodist Church at the Methodist Theological School in Ohio. I have a PhD in political science and am a retired elder in the UMC, having served Methodist churches in the UK and US. My writing is inspired by nature, and more recently the mindful meditation process of training for half-marathons.'

June McAllister: An Iona Community associate member ageing into God in the solitude of East Galway.

Barbara Miller is a retired minister within the United Church of Canada and is blessed to live in beautiful northern Ontario, where she and her husband, Brent, also farm cattle. They have three grown children and three grandchildren. Barb continues to support the work of the larger church and is currently in the creation stage of a resource for families, *Faith on the Move.*

James Munro: 'I was born in a Fife mining village, and so Scots was my native language. After a working life spent teaching French at university level I am now retired, and a member of Alva Parish Church, where from time to time I contribute pieces in Scots and English for the choir to sing.'

John Murning: 'Minister, Sherwood Greenlaw in Paisley. Married to Linda, overworked and underpaid.'

Avis Palmer has led Quiet Days for Retreat House Chester and is a Methodist Local Preacher.

Sarah Pascoe: 'I'm an ex-nurse, mother and grandmother. I love to live beside the sea.'

Mel Perkins writes as a way to work through life's ups and downs and changes. She loves combining creativity and spirituality, particularly in working alongside others, and lives in Victoria, Australia.

Janet Pybon is a Methodist minister who is passionate about encouraging churches to be fully inclusive, since she believes that God's love is intended for all people. In her free time she loves to be in the countryside or by the coast, enjoying the variety and beauty of God's natural world.

Margaret Roe is a retired Methodist minister living near Lincoln. She still has an active ministry, preaching and teaching, and has recently self-published two books: *Courage, Risk and Challenge: Women of the Old Testament Tell Their Stories* (volumes 1 and 2).

Sue Sabbagh has written poems since childhood, some of which have appeared in print or been broadcast on the BBC. She has a degree in English from Cambridge (Girton) and a Certificate in Religious Studies from Birkbeck College, London, is a wife, mother and grandmother.

Rev'd. Sr. Sandra Sears CSBC is a Local Priest in the Anglican Diocese of Willochra in rural South Australia, and a member of the Community of Sts Barnabas and Cecilia. As well as writing poetry, stories and liturgical resources, she is a composer of songs and hymns.

Robert Shooter: 'Throughout a career in social work and hospital chaplaincy, married life with Philippa and our four children, and now grandchildren, I have pursued creative writing and music. Born in Worksop, Nottinghamshire, I have studied, worked and lived in London, Wales, Lancashire and Yorkshire.'

Thom M Shuman is an associate member of the Iona Community living and writing in Columbus, OH.

Spill the Beans is 'a lectionary-based resource with a Scottish flavour for Sunday Schools, Junior Churches and worship leaders': http://spillbeans.org.uk

George Stuart is a lay member of the Toronto NSW Uniting Church of Australia congregation. He has written over 500 sets of new lyrics to well-known traditional church melodies, self-published in seven volumes of *Singing a New Song*. He was an ordained minister in the Uniting Church of Australia.

Jan Sutch Pickard is a poet, preacher and storyteller living on Mull. She is a former Warden of Iona Abbey and Ecumenical Accompanier. Her books and many resources include *Out of Iona: Words from a Crossroads of the World* and *Between High and Low Water: Sojourner Songs* (Wild Goose).

Evelyn Sweerts lives in Luxembourg with her husband Michael, four children and assorted pets. She is currently a pastoral assistant and expects to be ordained in the Church of England in 2019.

Kira Taylor: 'I'm a journalism student with a passion for social justice and writing. Most of my inspiration comes from a long period of illness, which God brought me through.'

Simon Taylor is a Baptist minister with a church in central Exeter and chapel just outside the city. He is also Baptist chaplain to the University of Exeter. Spring is his favourite season and he believes you can never plant enough spring bulbs.

Fiona van Wissen has volunteered with the Iona Community and the L'Arche Community in Rome. She is programme coordinator at Crieff Hills Retreat Centre in Canada and teaches outdoor education.

Jenny Wilson is Canon Precentor of St Peter's Cathedral in Adelaide, South Australia. She loves writing and preaching sermons, listening to the stories of members of her community and singing with the cathedral choir.

Index of authors

Gill Bailey 311
Ruth Bamforth 36
Ruth Bowen 157
James Hart Brumm 57, 58, 81, 84, 89, 92, 96, 102, 108, 113, 119, 124, 185, 212, 283, 285, 289, 305, 309
Ruth Burgess 15, 30, 52, 66, 70, 73, 94, 100, 101, 105, 110, 111, 131, 154, 171, 176, 192, 216, 244, 249, 257, 268, 275, 293, 332

Elizabeth Clark 218
David J.M. Coleman 136
Roddy Cowie 32, 107, 158, 184, 240, 318, 324
Kathy Crawford 18, 25, 148, 150, 187, 236, 255
Tricia Creamer 152
Liz Crumlish 83, 88, 118, 189, 210, 306

Judy Dinnen 18, 38
Carol Dixon 142, 151, 160, 263
Marjorie Dobson 24, 201

Chris Elgood 161

Brian Ford 272, 288, 304
Sally Foster-Fulton 52
Katherine Fox 79, 134
Ian M Fraser 128, 314

Kathy Galloway 43, 64, 168
Terry Garley 146, 162, 314
Louise Gough 31, 151, 213, 214, 254
Liz Gregory-Smith 163, 321

Carla Grosch-Miller 282

Roddy Hamilton 180, 190, 205, 218, 256
Mary Hanrahan 43, 142, 271, 305, 325
Catherine Harkin 240, 299
Pam Hathorn 28
J Mary Henderson 246

Judith Jessop 266, 280, 282

Tina Kemp 233
Janet Killeen 258, 278, 326

S Anne Lawson 200
Robin List 320
Iris Lloyd 267
Jo Love 72, 80, 87, 121, 178, 264, 269, 291

Rebeka Maples 20
June McAllister 324
Barbara Miller 147
James Munro 226
John Murning 74, 91, 169

Avis Palmer 71, 149, 166, 167, 198, 238
Sarah Pascoe 21
Mel Perkins 290, 319
Janet Pybon 146, 168, 315, 316

Margaret Roe 69

Sue Sabbagh 160, 277
Sr. Sandra Sears CSBC 237, 266, 278, 322

Robert Shooter 326
Thom M Shuman 42, 45, 56, 60, 133, 202, 211, 248, 274
Spill the Beans 78, 86, 88, 95, 123, 140, 181, 232, 309
George Stuart 318
Jan Sutch Pickard 19, 115, 156
Evelyn Sweerts 29

Kira Taylor 137
Simon Taylor 156, 182, 310, 322, 328

Fiona van Wissen 134, 270, 288

Jenny Wilson 44